Befriending Bipolar

A patient's perspective

Befriending Bipolar

A patient's perspective

By

Oliver Seligman

The author of this book does not dispense medical advice or prescribe the use of any technique as a form of treatment for physical, mental, or emotional problems without the advice of a physician, either directly or indirectly. The information in this book is not a substitute for and is not to be relied on for medical or healthcare professional advice. Please consult your doctor before changing, stopping, or starting any medical treatment. The author and publishers disclaim, as far as the law allows, any liability arising directly or indirectly from the information in this book.

The intent of the author is only to offer information of a general nature regarding his own experiences. In the event you use any information in this book for yourself, which is your constitutional right, the author and publisher assume no responsibility for your actions. So far as the author is aware the information given is correct and up to date as at 1/05/2021.

The material in this book may not be reproduced or transmitted in whole or in part in any medium (whether electronic, mechanical, or otherwise) without the express written authorization of Oliver Seligman (the author and publisher) except in the case of brief quotations embodied in critical articles and reviews.

To request authorization, please contact Oliver Seligman (oliverseligman@gmail.com).

Because of the dynamic nature of the Internet, any web addresses or links contained in this book may be changed since publication and may no longer be valid. The views expressed in this work are solely those of the author. Where permission was not attained, the names of the people in this book have been changed.

Also, by Oliver Seligman

The Broker who Broke Free

No Rest for the Wicked

CONTENTS

For my lovely wife, my loving mother and my laughter-filled father. Your compassion, patience and humour have made all the difference in the world.

Prologue

One hell of a shock

"Here's to the crazy ones. The misfits. The rebels. The troublemakers. The round pegs in the square holes. The ones who see things differently. They're not fond of rules. And they have no respect for the status quo. You can quote them, disagree with thcm, glorify or vilify them. About the only thing you can't do is ignore them. Because they change things. They push the human race forward. And while some may see them as the crazy ones, we see genius. Because the people who are crazy enough to think they can change the world, are the ones who do."

– Rob Siltanen, Advertising CEO.

An hour ago, I was taking a dip in the sea and now I am lying in bed, exhausted. The short walk to the harbour and the swim that followed was too much for me. A pounding headache and a cold sweat is the price I pay for trying to live a normal life. Why does everything I do go wrong?

Spring in Oslo arrives about two months later than most of its inhabitants would like and when it comes, the city and surrounding countryside spring to life. Five months of unforgiving winter days are over. The sun is no longer a distant, grey orb, teasing a winter hardened populace through snow-filled clouds. It has real warmth to it. Right on cue, eager snowdrops push their way out of the ground, daffodils follow and green leaves uncurl. It is spring and a day or two of minus ten doesn't change this fact at all. A short, one-sided battle ensues, but the power of spring prevails and people begin to smile again. The Norwegians are over the moon. Outwardly, they don't make a big fuss, for this is not their way, but inwardly they are high-fiving and running down the street in their underwear. Spring lasts a month or two at most and then there's a glorious summer to enjoy.

I usually spend my summers on a small island tucked away in the Oslo Fjord, where I live the Scandinavian dream of bathing, barbecues and hygging. We don't have a word for hygging in English, but it means to relax and do cosy things with the people we love. For the past two years I have been too ill to enjoy hygging or any other part of my life.

I was diagnosed with bipolar when I was seventeen and prescribed a psychiatric drug called lithium, which I took every day for nearly twenty years. It has now been three months since I weaned myself off lithium, but it hasn't been going well. So why have I committed one of society's cardinal sins and come off my medication? Well, it is because the side effects became too heavy to bear. As each year passed, the pain in my body mounted and my world shrank. I had been stable for years and wanted to see if I could manage without lithium. Perhaps I had even beaten bipolar? Or outgrown it? I bravely, or foolishly, or understandably lowered my dose and although this process was hellish, the end is now in sight. The experts have told me that once I have been off lithium for a couple of weeks my health will begin to improve. This is far from the truth.

These days I spend a lot of time crying and lying in bed. My standard of living is lower than it has ever been and everything about my life hurts. Yet if I keep going, if I can hold on and get through the withdrawals, I will be side-effect free and live the rest of my days a happy and healthy man. I hope.

My thoughts are interrupted by my wife coming in to check on me.

"Baby, how's it going," she asks, stroking my head. My fearful eyes meet hers and I am about to groan a reply when...

Zzuupp!

...In a blink, I'm transported from my bed to a sheltered harbour on another part of the island. I can see small cottages, hear gulls squawking and feel a soft breeze on my cheeks. As if by magic all of my pain leaves me. Had I not been so shocked by my first ever spontaneous teleportation, I might have appreciated the beauty of this scene, but instead I wonder what the hell is going on. The colours, the smells, the landscape; this place is as real as real life, perhaps more so. I am not dreaming or imagining this place. I am here! I am conscious, looking out of my own eyes, but I don't have a body and I'm floating thirty feet up in the air.

That is when I spot them, five monstrous looking creatures walking out of the sea, saltwater dripping from their scaley, grey skin. They are short, squat, ugly looking beasts and are carrying what look like oversized ray-guns from an early episode of Star Trek. They are silent, save for the odd mutter in an unkind language that is incomprehensible to me. As if by magic, I know why they have come. They are on a mission. A mission which has propelled them light years across the Galaxy to our tiny world. This alien hit squad is searching for someone and their lives depend on finding him. This someone is the most important individual in existence, the key to the age-old battle between good and evil. They are looking for the Messiah and they do not wish to pay him homage. These malevolent creatures don't want to help him, nor do they want to bow down at his feet and confess their sins. No, they want to kill him and they want to do it soon. The Messiah is the only man who can defeat their evil empire and end their wicked plans of universal domination. Every day his strength grows and their likelihood of success diminishes, so time is of the essence.

Smelling blood and sensing they are closing in on their prey, they speed march up a hill towards an old wooden house. Each clumsy step squeezes a muffled squelch from the base of their feet, as their short, squat legs pad up and down like frenzied Stormtroopers.

"Squwarg, glip, glip, awwwwk," grunts the leader, the slimy skin around his mouth folding awkwardly as he barks out each syllable. These creatures are not used to making casual conversation, preferring to remain absorbed in their thoughts of intergalactic conquest.

"Yaaaaakkkk," replies one of the group and the others nod. Despite the seriousness of their lethal mission, they have the appearance of cartoon characters. Everything about them; from their wart covered skin, to their oversized, fish shaped mouths and sharp reptilian teeth, is exaggerated and somehow comical. They are unaware of my presence as they squelch their way towards the house, the same house I was lying in a few minutes before. Or perhaps I'm still lying there? I can't be sure. The time and space travel of a bipolar psychosis has no respect for the rules of natural law.

"Squuuch, rrraaaa, aaakkk," the leader roars at one of his soldiers, spit flying from his mouth.

"Chuuuuuck," mutters the beast indignantly and is rewarded with a ray-gun butt to the side of his head. Enough! It is time to capture the man whose miserable life they have vowed to end.

One would think the Messiah would hear them approaching or at least have a legion of angelic warriors standing guard around him, but he doesn't. One would also think he would know he was the Messiah, the most vital cog in the known universe, but he doesn't. He has no idea at all. Not an inkling, until that moment, when finally, it dawns on me.

Holy shit! I am the Messiah. They're coming for me!

Introduction

"Manic-depression distorts moods and thoughts, incites dreadful behaviors, destroys the basis of rational thought and too often erodes the desire and will to live. It is an illness that is biological in its origins, yet one that feels psychological in the experience of it, an illness that is unique in conferring advantage and pleasure, yet one that brings in its wake almost unendurable suffering and, not infrequently, suicide."

– Kay Redfield Jamison, clinical psychologist and author.

In 1980, manic depression was renamed bipolar affective mood disorder, or bipolar for short. Bipolar is an illness which causes a person to experience both the ecstatic highs of mania and the dreadful lows of depression. The frequency and depth of these episodes varies greatly and at present there is no known cure.[1] Bipolar kills tens of thousands of people each year and on more than one occasion it has nearly killed me. The majority of people who die from bipolar do so through suicide,[2] although the risks of injury or death from an accident are significant for someone who is manic. The United States National Institute of Mental Health identifies three types of bipolar disorder:

- **Bipolar one disorder:** Defined by manic episodes which last at least seven days, or by manic symptoms that are so severe the person needs hospital care. Usually, depressive episodes occur as well, typically lasting at least two weeks. Episodes of depression with mixed features (depressive and manic symptoms at the same time) are possible, as are psychotic episodes.

- **Bipolar two disorder:** Defined by a pattern of depressive and hypomanic (mild mania) episodes, but not the full-blown manic episodes typical of bipolar one. There can be psychotic episodes, but they are usually less prevalent than in bipolar one.

- **Cyclothymic disorder or cyclothymia:** A milder type of bipolar with both hypomanic and milder depressive episodes which last for at least two years. This type of bipolar is less well known than the other two.

This book tells the story of my experiences with bipolar one, warts and all. I was diagnosed nearly thirty years ago and have spent time in mental hospitals in Scotland, Australia and Norway. I have been prescribed many types of medication and tried many forms of alternative treatments. Throughout this book, I have done my best to be as honest as possible, although I have changed the names of some of those involved. Some of my stories are embarrassing, but I have discovered mental illness is seldom pretty. I hope that by telling them, I can give others the chance to forgive themselves for their own embarrassing stories.

Experiencing bipolar isn't always dignified. When our minds lose touch with reality and our everyday emotions explode and become a source of almost infinite suffering, there is nowhere to hide. Life becomes torture and every part is affected; from finances to friendships, relationships to physical health. Bipolar is known for leaving a trail of destruction in its wake and an episode can take months to recover from. Many people don't know too much about this illness and throw around words like "manic" and "depressed" without knowing what they *really* mean. I hope to give a comprehensive insight into what mania, depression and psychosis *really* are and reveal what has helped and hindered me in my quest to live a good life. The terms mania and psychosis are defined below:

- **Mania:** An acute episode of delusion, excitement, overexuberance and grandeur which may last from a week to many months. A person may feel uncontrollably elated and very high in energy. They can be impulsive, restless, sleepless, talkative, uninhibited, irritable and have an unusually inflated sense of self-confidence and self-importance. Their sex drive may increase and they are more likely to take risks without considering the consequences. Thinking is rapid and flighty and their speech is fast and difficult to interrupt.

More serious symptoms can be hallucinations (auditory, visual, or olfactory) delusional thoughts and paranoia. Religious and sexual preoccupations are common. Patients can be rash, intrusive, aggressive and at times violent and they may need hospital treatment. Paranoia and delusions of grandeur or persecution are often present. [3]

- **Psychosis:** This condition is characterised by an impaired relationship with reality and is a serious mental disorder. People who are experiencing psychosis may have hallucinations, delusions or both. Sometimes a person with severe episodes of mania or depression may experience psychotic symptoms. These symptoms tend to correspond with the nature of the person's extreme mood. For example:

People having psychotic symptoms during a manic episode may believe they are famous, have a lot of money, or possess special powers.

People having psychotic symptoms during a depressive episode may believe they are financially ruined and penniless, have committed a crime, or have an unrecognised serious illness. [4]

No one is entirely sure as to what causes bipolar. Genetics are thought to play an important part, [5] although no single gene has been identified as the carrier. Childhood trauma is also considered to be a significant risk factor. [6]

A person who is mentally ill will often look normal, but they won't feel it. It is easy to see when someone has a broken leg, but a person with bipolar may show no outward signs of illness. People with bipolar tend to have "up and down" personalities, which can make it more challenging to see that they are mentally ill. The average person isn't afraid of a broken leg, but many are scared of mental illness. This fear adds to the stigma which often comes with a mental disorder, compounding the challenges around it for both the sufferer and those around her.

Anyone can develop bipolar, but the majority are young, imaginative and gifted. The average age of onset is twenty-five, although it can affect younger people and those in their fifties too. [7] Bipolar is unique, in that it can bring out the best and the worst in us. It can lead to ecstasy or suicide, creativity or apathy, success beyond our wildest dreams or abject failure.

At present, medication is the most widespread treatment, but it can come at a cost. My medication allows me to be happy and at peace, but puts a significant strain on my body and my mind. For others, the meds don't work, or the side effects are unbearable, leaving them to look elsewhere for the answers. Mental illness is a lottery. What works and what doesn't work, seems to vary from one individual to the next and each person's journey has its own unique twists, turns, peaks and pits.

There is hope. New treatments are on offer, research is finding answers and society is becoming more compassionate in the way it views mental illness. I hope this book will ease the burden on readers who live with bipolar or depression and help their friends and family to understand them and their disorder better. I also hope it will offer the psychiatric world an insightful perspective into this illness. Finally, I hope that one day soon prolonged mental illness and suffering will be consigned to the history books.

Chapter 1. I never asked for this

"Bipolar robs you of that which is you. It can take from you the very core of your being and replace it with something that is completely opposite of who and what you truly are... I no longer could tell reality from fantasy, and I walked in a world no longer my own."

– Alyssa Reyans, Letters from a Bipolar Mother.

"How long have you been here?" the gaunt, unshaven man asked the lady sitting next to me, his fingers tapping the table too fast for my liking. He had a feral, haunted look in his eyes and the smell of rotting eggs hung around him like an unwanted guest. The three of us sat on hard plastic chairs around a hard plastic table in the hospital canteen. The canteen was far from welcoming; white walls, white chairs, white tables, metal sinks and kitchen staff who looked like they would have chewed off their arms to be somewhere else. On nearby tables, other patients picked at their flavourless food in silence or pushed it around their plates with no intention of letting it anywhere near their mouths.

It was my first breakfast as an inpatient in the Royal Edinburgh Psychiatric Hospital and it was not a meal I would ever want to repeat. I was seventeen and felt like a calf separated from the herd, surrounded by strangers who bristled with madness. Strong sedatives had taken the edge off my paranoia, but I was in no state to talk. Maggie, the lady sitting next to me, filled the silence. Maggie was a white-haired pensioner who looked like she had spent her entire life drunk, but hadn't enjoyed a drop. For the last twenty minutes, she had talked about her journey through the Scottish mental health system, rarely drawing breath. Forty years in and out of psychiatric institutes, Maggie had been around the block and was proud of it. She had seen it all and was at home amidst the screams and violence, which I was soon to discover were a part of everyday life in a mental hospital. I, on the other hand, was not old enough to order a pint and her tales filled me with dread.

"Nine months. I've got no idea when I'll get out," Maggie replied matter-of-factly, as if she was telling the gaunt man it was raining outside.

"Oh, my God," I thought. "What if I never get out?"

My heart hollowed, my stomach tightened and before I knew it, I was running towards a sink. I reached it in the nick of time, spewing liquid vomit all over it and the floor around. Once the retching was over, a mixture of embarrassment and loneliness hit me. The canteen was now silent and every patient who was capable of doing so was staring straight at me.

A kindhearted nurse rushed to my side and put a comforting hand on my back.

"It's okay, Oliver. It's not your fault. I'll clear this up," she reassured me in a soft voice, as she poked through my sick with the end of her biro, checking to see if my morning pills had been digested or not. It was the autumn of 1993, I had barely eaten or slept for two weeks and was in the grip of a deep and horrifying manic psychosis.

Things had started to go wrong eight months earlier, in the lead up to the Easter holidays before my A-level exams. Since I was little, I had a personality that was highly-strung. I was up and down; one moment positive, enthusiastic and hyperactive; anxious, impatient and irritated the next. Charming and quick witted, I had a fast and creative mind and was socially confident. I found it easy to engage groups of people, to hold their attention and make them laugh. I was also a Mummy's boy, nervous and afraid, and lacking in the confidence that seemed to shine from me on social occasions.

As the beginnings of my first mania began to take hold, my extrovert qualities shone brighter and my fears vanished in a puff of over-confident smoke. I became overbearing; enamoured with my own ideas and very pleased with myself. My mind speeded up and I slept less. It was a time when I needed to make plans for my future, but most of them were ludicrously optimistic and detached from reality. I felt superhuman and had boundless reserves of energy, bouncing out of bed in the morning and spending the whole day feeling on top of the world. My parents noticed how happy I was, but had no reason to worry about me. Most parents don't consider having a happy teenager in the house to be a big problem.

There developed a kind of spirituality to the way I viewed the world. All of life was intrinsically interconnected and a sense of awe and wonder hung over everything. I felt I had been given access to a part of creation that others were oblivious to, which made me feel special indeed. I tried to explain my strange, cosmic ideas to my friends, but no one understood. This didn't discourage me, quite to the contrary, I pitied their primitive intellects. I talked and talked and talked, unaware of when to give others space. My relentless enthusiasm and excess energy was tiresome for everyone around me, but I didn't care because I was caught in the current of a euphoric mania. Those days flew by with a laughter, busyness and chaos I considered normal. However, life had no intention of letting me stay in that blissful state for long.

After the holidays, I returned to boarding school completely unprepared for my exams, having not revised at all. I had ignored this academic necessity by convincing myself I was a genius. My cocksure attitude was one of many symptoms of a mania that would last for over half a year.

On my first day back at school reality caught up with me. I had less than a week before my first exam and I hadn't opened a textbook in a month. Overnight my mania transformed from euphoria into a fearful, stuttering, snowballing panic. I threw myself into cramming, staying up late into the night using hypnosis tapes to force facts into my head. My memory was unusually poor, so I pushed myself harder, forcing information into my brain whilst steadily becoming more stressed out.

My classmates seemed to handle the pressure well, but I was a nervous wreck. Like an agitated ferret, I got faster and faster, running around in circles chasing my tail. I blurted out offensive comments at the wrong moments, not caring if I hurt people's feelings. I had never been known for my tact, but the sense of humour I relied upon to smooth my outbursts had disappeared. I wasn't charming or funny anymore, I was crass and abrasive. A bout of mania had invaded my mind and because it had never happened before, I had no idea I was soon to be possessed by it.

Over the course of the summer term my speech quickened, as did my thoughts. My still unidentified illness gained momentum and I morphed into someone my friends hardly recognised. Thoughts and ideas bounced around my head like a pinball machine and I found it impossible to hold a conversation without jumping from one topic to another. My insecurities deepened and I became extremely negative. I couldn't settle, I lost weight and there was a desperation about me, as if an unseen force was taking me over and twisting me into someone I didn't want to be. Everything needed to be done right now and it was never good enough.

Ever since I could remember, anxious periods had been a part of my life, but now anxiety was my constant companion. My mind, which a few weeks before had been filled with optimism, was tearing me down, telling me I was worthless and going to fail. My friends were patient, but I pushed their patience to the limit and some of those friendships never recovered. There is only so much mania a friendship can take before it falls apart. I didn't think to ask anyone for help because I didn't think there was anything wrong with me. I just ploughed on.

Once my A-levels were over I should have felt a sense of relief, but it never came. I went back home to Scotland, but still I couldn't relax. Ordinarily, I loved being at home and spent a great deal of time outdoors: walking the dogs, working in the garden, running or otherwise entertaining myself. This time the activities which used to relax me no longer could and even though I was in the perfect place to unwind, I couldn't. I got a part time job at a local petrol station, but had to give it up after my manic mind made it problematic to work. My poor parents had to deal with an uptight, uncooperative and humourless son who felt like he could explode at any second. Like an old pressure cooker with the heat turned up, something had to give.

My parents thought a bit of time at home would give me the chance to calm down, but the mania began to morph into a psychosis. I started to imagine fictitious scenarios which had nothing to do with real life and became consumed by an irrational fear that the CIA was following me. I felt like a hunted animal. Unable to rest. Unable to stop running. As time went on, the episode continued to develop, refusing to tread water for too long. One day, I would see the world as an exquisite expression of divinity, cascading with bright, blazing colours. The next I would wake up on a damaged planet; the trees were dying, the people depressed and the world a prison full of suffering and hate.

After a trip to my local swimming baths, my state of mind took a turn for the worse. At the pool I had got chatting to a bubbly, fifteen-year-old girl and once we had finished swimming she asked me to drive her home. I remember sitting beside her in the car wanting to kiss her, but nothing happened. For years, I had carried around an irrational fear of going to prison for a crime I didn't commit. I would sometimes wake up in the middle of the night sweating, as I searched my memory for who I had assaulted the day before.

Over the following days my innocent meeting with the girl at the swimming pool, she became the focus of a paranoid psychosis, the likes of which I had never experienced. Although nothing untoward had happened, I was overcome with guilt and petrified that she was going to accuse me of raping her. Every time the phone or the doorbell rang, I panicked, believing it was the police coming for me. The psychosis twisted everything out of proportion, but I didn't dare to tell a soul because I felt like such a deviant. When I lay in bed at night, staring into the blackness behind my eyelids, a fierce fear chipped away at my dwindling sanity and I cried myself to sleep.

It all came to a head when I went on a camping holiday in Cornwall with friends from school. Five young men, late nights, girls, beer and surfing was not what I needed. My mother told me it was a bad idea, but I went anyway. When I turned up at the campsite, my friends noticed I was too skinny and couldn't relax. I talked astonishingly fast and although it annoyed them, I couldn't stop myself. On the first evening, I dared two of my friends to hold onto my ankles and dangle me headfirst from the top of a hundred-foot cliff. It was exhilarating. As I hung there, listening to the sound of the waves crashing below, I felt better than I had done in months. This stunt disengaged my brutal mind, but once back on *terra firma* it returned with a vengeance.

As the holiday went on, my behaviour took a nosedive and I became more erratic and difficult to be around. I stole a friend's car and hid it in a corner of our campsite. When I eventually owned up, he didn't see the funny side. Rather than apologise, I angrily accused him of not being able to take a joke. The following day, I stole ten pounds from another friend's wallet and when questioned, I furiously denied knowing anything about it.

A-level results came out and to the great surprise of anyone who had witnessed my behaviour in the previous months, I got straight As. Out of character, I didn't bother to call my parents who had supported me all along. The swansong of this calamitous holiday occurred when I ripped up my train ticket home, proclaiming I intended to live in

Cornwall forever. Whatever was wrong with me was creating suffering in every part of my life, undermining my integrity, judgment and friendships. By the end of the holiday, my friends must have been relieved to see the back of me. I certainly would have been.

After a torrid week, I borrowed money for a train ticket home to Edinburgh. The mania had now developed into a full-blown, manic psychosis and the pressure inside my mind was unbearable. I knew I was falling apart, but I didn't know why. Sitting alone on the train, I broke. I had been holding it together for months, but was too exhausted to keep going. I went to the toilet, sat on the seat and bawled my eyes out in private. Scared of facing another six hours on the train, I got off at the next stop and stumbled into a British Transport Police station in floods of tears.

"My grandmother has killed herself," I told the policeman manning reception. This was true. My grandmother had taken her own life, but it had happened ten years before I was born. This meant nothing to the depression which was rearing its ugly head. It mixed with the mania and psychosis to create a truly disturbing experience. Later that day the policeman put me on a sleeper train back to Edinburgh.

My father picked me up at the railway station. I looked terrible and my fingers were scrunched up into claws, as if my hands were deformed by arthritis. They were stuck fast, so he had to buckle my seatbelt for me. Both of my parents suspected I had taken drugs in Cornwall, but my sister, a trainee nurse, could see I was manic. For the first time since the illness had surfaced, it became obvious that I was very ill, so my mother took me straight to the doctor. By a stroke of bad luck, my doctor was on holiday and I was seen by a *locum*.

"Please give me some sleeping pills. I need to sleep," I told him. "If I can get some sleep, I'll be fine."

He wouldn't prescribe them.

"You're not psychotic," he replied. "You need some rest and you'll be fine. A-levels are a stressful time."

"Without sleeping pills, I won't get any rest," I argued, but he didn't believe me.

That night I lay in bed awake for hours, tossing and turning. Whenever I began to settle, my body would jump as a fearful thought startled me awake. I would then spring out of bed in a panic and pace around the house for half an hour. The more I wanted to sleep, the less I slept. The less I slept, the more uptight I became. The more uptight I became, the less I could sleep. This cycle repeated itself for the following two nights, with my frantic mother exhausted from keeping an eye on me.

The lack of sleep added to my feelings of desperation and paranoia. One morning, when I was brushing my teeth, I spotted a speck of dirt around the rim of the plughole. I was petrified that the sink's lethal bacteria would kill me and my parents. Other old fears or shameful things I had done as a child, vied for my attention. I looked pale and my body was unnaturally tense; my hands still twisted into grotesque claws. I would lie in bed staring at the ceiling, holding my tightly clenched "lobster claws" aloft, whilst drawing peculiar patterns with them in the air. My parents' comforting words made no difference to me. I needed professional help. What I wished for more than anything was a quiet hospital bed where I could sleep. If only I could get some sleep, I would be fine.

Learnings:

1. Mental illness can creep up slowly and be hard to detect. I was ill for some time before anyone, including myself, realised what was happening.

2. My "up and down" personality made it harder to spot that I was ill, as did the fact that it was my first episode.

3. When I was manic, the activities which usually relaxed me no longer did. There seemed to be nothing I could do to calm myself down or stop the illness developing.

Chapter 2. Hell exists between our ears

"Without love, our earth is a tomb."

– Robert Browning, Poet and Playwright.

My mother and I walked into the main hall of Edinburgh's biggest mental hospital, avoiding making eye contact with the shifty looking characters who were smoking by the entrance. They were unshaven, scruffily dressed and rough around the edges, with a tribal air about them. The type of people who I imagined wandered around the park talking to themselves over a can of Special Brew. A tall, wiry man with yellow eyes stared at me with menace, or at least that was how my paranoid mind saw him. As I caught his gaze, he lurched forward clumsily. For a brief moment I thought he was going to attack us, but he muttered something under his breath, threw his cigarette onto the tarmac and turned away.

We followed the signs to ward number two and once we got there, we sat down in a cramped waiting room. The white walls, polished floors and heavy steel doors reminded me of a prison and I shuddered. A metal lock clanged and somewhere in the distance a troubled woman screamed, making me jump. This place wasn't a hospital; it *was* a prison. I was sure of it. As I looked around fervently, I was struck by the sights, sounds and smells of madness. A group of disturbing characters rocked back and forth, as they sat on old flea-bitten sofas, muttering to themselves. Others stomped around the corridors, teeth clenched, ready to explode. Yet more looked dazed, like heavily medicated zombies masquerading as people. They moved with a sinister clumsiness, their arms flailing in slow motion, as if they were wading through thick syrup. A tattooed man wandered into the waiting room and started to bellow at the top of his voice for no apparent reason. This drew the attention of two burly security guards, who approached him with caution. They spoke softly, but he ended up lying face down on the floor in an arm lock, shouting obscenities until he ran out of steam. Then I *really knew* it was a prison.

An undercover policeman, posing as a young hospital consultant, ushered us into his office. I didn't want to go in because I knew he would try to trick me into confessing that I had raped the girl at the swimming pool. If I kept quiet, he wouldn't be able to get any evidence out of me. However, if I gave him anything more than a simple "yes" or a "no," he would lock me up and throw away the key. Understandably, the consultant decided I wasn't well enough to go home and should be admitted to ward two for further assessment.

My mother had packed an overnight bag for me, but I was determined not to unzip it. My wish for a hospital bed had come true, but a bed in ward two was a nightmare I couldn't face. This undercover policeman was going to lock me up with these terrifying people and I could do nothing about it. Never in my life had I felt so claustrophobic.

"I can't do this. I can't stay here," I thought, as I threw my mother a fearful look.

"I'm not leaving you here," she replied, reading my mind. Then began the onerous task of convincing the consultant I couldn't stay in ward two.

"I'm not leaving him here," she told him in a firm tone few young men could ignore; that of a determined mother protecting her child. The consultant's resolve weakened, but fearing I might be a danger to myself, he pushed a little harder for me to stay.

"Have you thought about hurting yourself?" he asked me.

I shook my head.

"Have you had suicidal thoughts?"

I shook my head again.

"I just want to sleep," I replied, hoping I hadn't incriminated myself. The consultant looked at my mother, paused and then decided he wasn't going to win this battle.

"Okay, Oliver. You can go home," he nodded deliberately. "I'll speak to a psychiatrist at the Young People's Unit and someone will call you tomorrow."

Another sleepless night followed, but then a glimmer of hope appeared on the horizon. A psychiatrist from the Young People's Unit (YPU) called and told us she had found a bed for me in ward one. Ward one was a smaller ward used for mothers with babies and young children. Patients who couldn't cope with the larger wards, were sometimes lucky enough to get a bed there too. I had no idea at the time, but I was fortunate to get into ward one, which in terms of mental health was the equivalent of the Ritz.

On my first day in ward one, I was prescribed two medicines: Haloperidol and Diazepam. Haloperidol is an antipsychotic or downer, designed to bring patients out of psychosis and calm their manic minds. Diazepam is a sleeping pill, an opiate which delivers a blissful sensation before knocking you out. Thanks to Diazepam, I fell into the deep slumber I had been praying for for weeks. The gift of sleep was a huge relief, but my mania had progressed so far that sleep alone wasn't enough to heal me, so I was given Haloperidol. My first dose of Haloperidol hit me like a missile. It soon weakened my psychotic mania, but plunged me into the depths of the deepest depression imaginable. A place the likes of which I had never experienced before.

- **Depression:** A common mental health problem which causes people to experience low mood, loss of interest or pleasure, feelings of guilt, disturbed sleep or appetite, low energy and poor concentration.

Symptoms may vary, but generally encompass a feeling of sadness, hopelessness or despair. These can include: a sadness which doesn't go away, difficulty concentrating, an inability to enjoy things that are usually pleasurable or interesting, feeling anxious all the time, avoiding other people, feelings of helplessness and hopelessness, finding it hard to function, thinking about suicide, death and self-harm. Depression's symptoms can vary in severity, from mild, to moderate, to severe. [8]

Psychiatry by its nature involves experimentation, which means finding the right medication and dosage is often a case of trial and error. No one anticipated how badly I would react to Haloperidol. It sent me to a place I can only describe as the lower reaches of hell, where no sense of hope, goodness, life or pleasure existed. A heavy cloak of endless misery was thrown over my head and I became suicidal, loathing myself with every ounce of my being. A fog of despair suffocated me with hopelessness, as it whispered hatred in my ear. I had nothing to live for and no hope that my suffering would ever end.

I was caught in the jaws of a medication-induced depression, an indescribably awful place to be. All sense of time vanished, which meant I was trapped in this horrifying experience forever. I had no idea if ten minutes, three hours or three days had passed because my mind no longer worked. I couldn't muster any good memories to cheer me, or imagine a happy future to look forward to, just an eternity of pain. I whimpered, I moaned and I suffered, but nothing I could do changed any of it. Had I had the energy to kill myself, I would have tried. I would have done anything to end my suffering. For the best part of a month, I lay in bed all day, staring into space until I fell into the blessed relief of sleep at night.

Every morning at seven thirty, a nurse would come into my room and wake me. If I lay perfectly still, I had a second or two where I felt like myself again. Had it all been a bad dream? Like clockwork, the depression slithered back into my brain, making its home in the safe place I used to call "me." Like some hideous creature with a life of its own, it dragged me back into hell and there was not a thing I could do to stop it. Like the Greek King Tantalus, damned to an eternity of temptation with wine he couldn't drink and grapes he couldn't grasp, I was given a brief glimpse of normality, only for it to be taken away. This happened every morning for six weeks.

Haloperidol made my body tick and spasm. It hardened my muscles, making it difficult to move. I shuffled around like an old, deformed man and needed help to go to the toilet. Whenever I tried to eat, my appetite deserted me. I couldn't dress myself or watch television and if I tried to formulate words they wouldn't come out. All I could do was suffer; that was it. I had descended into a depressive stupor, physically paralysed by a psychological illness, unable to relate to anything around me. I believed the world was about to end and it was merely a matter of time before everyone I knew suffered a horrible demise. I lost the will to live and unconsciously began to starve myself to death.

One lunchtime my mother came to visit and found me sitting alone in my room, staring into space, with unchewed vegetables hanging out of my open mouth. I was too weak to chew. The depression had shut me down and if I did get close to swallowing anything, I was so disgusted with myself that I promptly retched it up. Mealtimes had become an ordeal, with my confidence declining, as I failed to eat again and again. It was soul destroying. In three weeks, I barely kept down a morsel of food.

The nurses could see the other patients were stressing me out and suggested I eat alone in my room, but that didn't work either. No matter how hard I tried I couldn't eat. The doctors reduced my dose of Haloperidol, but they didn't want to stop it altogether because it was stabilising my mania.

After two savage weeks, they took me off the drug, but I now needed antidepressants to lift me up. I couldn't start them immediately because the Haloperidol had to leave my system first, so I went cold turkey. The withdrawals were horrific. I lay in bed tossing and turning, twitching, sweating and spasming uncontrollably, my face almost unrecognisable even to my parents. The days were long, with nothing to do other than experience my body contort painfully and my mind go crazy with fear. A psychiatrist later told me that coming off Haloperidol was like coming off heroin, only worse.

Alongside the withdrawals, my eating problem was spiraling out of control. Before I became ill, my fighting weight was a modest ten stones. I had now lost more than two and a half. My cheeks looked hollow, my ribs protruded and when I stood up I had to grab my trousers to stop them falling off me. Still, I couldn't eat. The nurses gave me protein shakes, which I managed to keep down, but my weight kept dropping. The doctors decided that if this carried on much longer, they would have to force feed me through a nasal tube fed into my stomach. Their plan didn't encourage me to eat. Quite to the contrary, it piled on the pressure and the pressure made it harder to eat. Was there ever going to be an end to this nightmare?

Fourteen days after my final dose of Haloperidol, I began to take an antidepressant called Paroxetine. I swallowed a tiny, shiny, white, oval pill every morning, but for ten long days Paroxetine had no noticeable effect on my stupor. Like Atreyu in *The Never Ending Story,* I trudged through the swamp of sadness, with little hope I would ever reach the end. By now the doctors were considering other antidepressants and even electro convulsive therapy, but in the nick of time, one of the nurses noticed glimpses of my depression lifting. I uttered a few words which didn't involve me wanting to die and I could sit in a chair for longer than a minute without trying to go elsewhere. Thanks to her, the doctors kept faith with Paroxetine and I slowly began to edge my way back to life.

Then a miracle of sorts occurred. The day before I was due to be force fed, I was visited by a family friend. I remember Lel walking into my room. I was sitting at a desk in the corner, an untouched plate of food in front of me.

"It's all going to be okay, Ollie. You're going to get through this and be well again," Lel reassured me, her voice full of warmth. She reached into her handbag and took out a paper bag with four profiteroles in it. Handing me one of the roles she smiled. Cautiously, I took the chocolate covered pastry and placed it in my mouth, as if I had forgotten how to eat. Then I began to chew. I chewed slowly and deliberately, smelling the pastry and tasting its soft sweetness. After some time, I mustered up the courage to swallow.

Success!

The spell had been broken. I could eat again! I smiled for the first time in weeks.

"Every day in every way you're getting better and better," Lel told me with heartening confidence and I believed her. "You can say it to yourself in front of the mirror, every day if you like?"

For months, the first thing I did when I got out of bed in the morning, was stand in front of the mirror and repeat those magic words.

"Every day in every way I'm getting better and better." This mantra boosted my confidence and transformed me from feeling like a helpless victim, into someone who could do something positive to get well. Combined with the effect of Paroxetine, hell became misery and then misery became gloom and then gloom became tolerable, as I emerged from the depression. My recovery was too slow for my liking, but the doctors were pleased with my progress. Had I bounced back too quickly, I could easily have slipped back into mania again. As soon as I began to feel better, I started to joke with the hospital staff. As is usually the case with people who have seen the tougher sides of life, many of them had a great sense of humour and I became fond of them. They were warm, interested and genuinely cared about me and the other patients. Their company took my mind away from my problems and their compassion speeded my recovery.

The other patients on my ward were an eclectic bunch. One of them, a Jamaican woman called Amelia, shuffled up and down the corridors all day long in a state of depression. She had dark rings around bloodshot eyes and was on suicide watch, accompanied by a nurse who walked beside her all of the time. For the most part Amelia was silent, but every so often she would let out a bloodcurdling cry. I couldn't understand what she was saying, but her voice went right through me and I decided I didn't like her. One day Amelia's husband and two small children came to visit her. Her children were three and five years old and when she saw them, her lifeless eyes seemed to light up, but she wasn't well enough to give them a hug. Instead, they clung to her dress vying for their mother's attention, but got none. It was the saddest sight I had ever seen and my dislike for Amelia vanished in a wave of sympathy.

Jane, a seventeen-year-old woman with anorexia nervosa was also a patient on the ward. She had an angelic look about her, but was too shy and depressed to speak. She had tried to kill herself and tiptoed around the ward avoiding looking anyone in the eye. Jane had an elegance few possess and was so thin she could have floated away. The last place in the world I would have pictured her was in a mental ward. Yet here she was. Life had somehow conspired to give her an illness of the mind and an indefinite stay in a place she would never have chosen to be. When I looked closer at Jane's arms, I could see an army of swollen, pink cut marks. These permanent reminders of her troubled mind looked out of place on someone so beautiful. I wanted to talk to Jane, but I never did.

The ward was also a temporary home to a heart surgeon, an investment banker, a musician and other patients who struggled to hold down any kind of job. Mental illness is an incredible leveler and although we all came from different backgrounds, we were all treated with the same respect.

I like to find humour in the darker parts of life. Although I didn't find anything funny when I was ill, When I look back there were some funny things happening in in ward one. As Amelia walked the corridors, letting out the occasional bloodcurdling scream, she also let out equally bloodcurdling farts. Jane, the most unlikely person to act inappropriately in public, did the same; wandering around the ward, oblivious to the fact that her bottom was belching out noxious gases. I hated the smell, but after a couple of days on Haloperidol, I became a member of their not so prestigious club, pumping out powerful sulphurous smells into the ward. It was the same stench of rotten eggs which had surrounded the gaunt, unshaven man who I met on my first day. It was catalysed by the medication we all took. How the nurses survived this chemical onslaught, I will never know.

The times when, as part of my psychosis, I believed I was a black panther, also now make me chuckle. I was not *any* black panther. I was *the* alpha male on the block. Two hundred pounds of taut, feline magnificence, whose task was to assert his authority over the rest of the ward. Late at night, when it was pitch black, save for a weak glow coming from the emergency exit signs, I prowled around the corridors in my pajamas, dressing gown and slippers. All eight skinny stones of adolescence surveying my jungle kingdom. If I met another patient, I would stop and stare them down. They were on my turf and needed to know who was boss. I was never outwardly aggressive towards anyone, but inside I felt fearsome. When the nurses found me, as they always did, they would gently guide me back to my room and I would follow meekly.

The visiting times on ward one were flexible, which meant my parents could visit me often. This made a huge difference to me. They both had busy lives and yet were able to see me twice a day. Their visits and hence the flexible visiting hours, made all the difference, speeding my recovery.

During the last few weeks of my stay, I was well enough to venture out of the hospital with them. We inevitably found our way to a local diner called Sherry's, where I would order a hot chocolate with squirty cream and two flakes poking out of the top. To this day I am still comforted by the taste of a thick, creamy hot chocolate.

After three months in the Royal Edinburgh Hospital, I was discharged, but was so used to living there I became anxious about going home. I felt safe in that strangely unpredictable environment, even when patients were screaming or security guards running. I had become attached to the staff and many of the patients and I knew once I left I would probably never see them again. When I walked out of the sliding glass doors for the last time, I can honestly say I was sad to leave. I looked over at the shifty looking characters who were smoking by the entrance. Most of them were now my friends.

Learnings:

1. There are different levels of depression a person can experience. All of which are deeply unpleasant and challenging (see Chapter six).

2. Families and friends can play an essential role in supporting patients with mental health problems and they should not underestimate the difference they can make.

3. Everything positive which happened to me in hospital, came from people who were kind and supportive. My mother's love got me a bed in ward one, Lel's kind words got me eating again, my parents visits and the hospital staff's support gave me faith I would recover.

4. Flexible visiting hours were a significant benefit. [9]

5. The sentence "every day in every way I'm getting better and better," gave me something I could do to improve my state of mind. It transformed me from being a man who was passively waiting to get well, to a man who could do something positive about it.

6. Mental hospitals can be intimidating, but as my health improved and I grew accustomed to the people and routines, I felt safer and more at home.

7. A few years after my stay in the Royal Edinburgh Hospital, an inpatient unit for teenagers was built in Southeast Scotland. One of the advantages of this is that the alarming encounters with long term adult patients that I experienced are avoided by young, vulnerable people.

Chapter 3. Going on medication

"It's not stress that kills us; it is our reaction to it."

– Hans Selye, Endocrinologist.

To medicate or not to medicate? That is the question; and one of the most controversial areas of mental illness. An area full of emotion, confusion, advice, opinions, choices, successes, failures and sometimes even suicide. It is not my place to encourage people to stay on their medication or to come off it, that is the realm of trained professionals. What I wish to do is to share my own experiences with bipolar and medication.

At seventeen, a huge stop sign fell from the sky and landed in front of me. Before bipolar, I didn't have a clue who I was, but after my first mania I had even less of an idea. The episode shook me to the core and left me unable to fully trust anything I thought, felt or said. Up until that point, my teenage life had been all about my friends, but this uninvited mental meteorite turned me upside down and inside out. My friends were moving forward with their lives, but I wasn't included and I didn't know if I ever would be. I had been left behind by the herd, no longer enjoying its protective security, which left me feeling lonely and lost.

I had planned to spend my Gap year (the year between school and university) in America, working at a children's camp, but when my first episode hit, I was forced to cancel. My long anticipated American adventure was no more and I had no choice other than to stay at home in Scotland. Although I was disappointed, a part of me was relieved. Had I flown to America it would not have gone well.

I thrive when I'm busy and have a purpose to move towards, but I was forced to live a far more sedate life than I wanted to. My plans had been demolished without warning and conjuring up a sense of purpose wasn't easy. Far from feeling one hundred percent, I drove into Edinburgh every week for an appointment with my new psychiatrist, a man called Dr. Rob Wrate. Dr. Wrate was sleight, with glasses and a beard and every time I saw him, he was wearing a smart, Harris tweed jacket. He was the spitting image of the psychiatrist played by Robin Williams in the film *Good Will Hunting* and similar in temperament. Dr. Wrate was friendly, smiled easily and his intelligent eyes danced when he spoke. We got on extremely well and it didn't take long for him to win my trust and respect. I cannot emphasise enough how helpful it was to have such a gifted psychiatrist in my corner and to meet with him regularly. I had a habit of trying to deal with my problems on my own, but sharing them with Dr. Wrate shone a light on them which I could never have done by myself.

He listened intently and didn't rush to conclusions or hurry with his advice. He was perceptive and talked to me in a way that ensured I properly understood his words.

Sometimes I saw him on my own and sometimes I took my mother along with me, because he made her feel better too!

Dr. Wrate took me off anti-depressants to see how I would cope without medication, but my mood didn't change much at all. Some days I felt like a caged tiger, others like a lost sheep and some like a sedated slug who could scarcely crawl his way through life. Many of my good qualities went into hibernation as I fell back into periods of mild depression, anxiety and boredom. I spent a lot of time alone, going for walks or lying on my bed dozing. Getting out of bed in the mornings was laborious, my appetite sparrow-like and the energy and motivation to rebuild my life non-existent.

My mother was willing to try anything that might aid my recovery and took me to see a Hypnotherapist in Edinburgh. When I left the Hypnotherapist's office, I couldn't believe my luck. In one appointment, she had calmed my anxiety and I felt more relaxed than I had done in years. I spent the afternoon wandering around the house, revelling my newfound inner calm. Unfortunately, the hypnotherapy was far from a permanent cure and later that day my anxiety rushed back, like a flash flood cascading down a parched valley. Sitting in my living room, I overheard my mother innocently telling my father that my appointment with the hypnotherapist had gone well.

"Oh shit! It was a set up," I panicked, as paranoid thoughts rushed into my mind. "She wasn't a real hypnotherapist. She was a government agent trying to brainwash me." Merely hearing the hypnotherapist's name was enough to reignite a state of paranoia and send me back to square one.

Emotional instability dominated my state of mind for months, but I kept putting one foot in front of the other, not least because I didn't have anything else to do. Gradually my mood started to improve and after a challenging year for both me and my parents, I went to Newcastle University hoping it would bring me back to life.

Academically, my first year was a write-off. From the beginning, I struggled to concentrate and only went to a handful of lectures. Trying to perform academically, whilst seeing the world through bipolar bifocals, wasn't easy. I handed in two poorly scribbled assignments, both of which failed to impress my lecturers. If it wasn't the worst work they had been forced to read, it wasn't far off it.

My saving grace was getting involved with the university's Officer Training Corps (OTC), which was a section of the Territorial Army. I passed selection and became a member of an organisation which gave me meaning, purpose and physical challenges. It was a great way to meet people and earn some extra pocket money and I thrived in the social and humorous environment the OTC embodied. Many of my peers were good people with good values who didn't take themselves too seriously. I fired automatic weapons, lived in the woods, abseiled headfirst off cliffs and competed in both rugby and judo. I charged around the countryside in state-of-the-art tanks and jumped out of perfectly good helicopters for fun. For a while these adventures lifted my mood, but as the gloomy Northeastern winter nights drew in, even the OTC was not enough to stop depression from knocking on my door. In the space of a couple of days, I went from happy, to holed up in my room weeping uncontrollably, my confidence shattered. I returned to Edinburgh, deflated, too ill to stay at university.

Sitting in Dr. Wrate's office in floods of tears, I explained that I had been holding myself together for months. In itself, university had not been particularly stressful, but bipolar had lowered my tolerance for stress to such a degree, that getting through the day sometimes felt like treading water with heavy weights strapped to my ankles. It was then I made a discovery. I discovered my stress levels didn't have as much to do with my circumstances as I had previously thought. They were heavily influenced by my state of mind. If I was happy and stable, I could take many of life's challenges in my stride, but when I felt uptight or fearful, the smallest things stressed me out.

In that first term, I also learned that, without medication or some extra help, I couldn't find permanent stability. Outside the excitement of the OTC, I tended to get disheartened and judgmental and I made few friends. I hated my mental fragility and the insecurity of not knowing if I was about to become ill or not. Both made me feel deeply unsafe. Bipolar was more persistent than I had first imagined. Like a silent assassin, it hovered in the background and as soon as something positive wandered into my life, it moved in to destroy it.

Since I had been in hospital, the fear of becoming ill again had never left me. The trauma of the episode had made me hypersensitive to what was going on inside my head. When I laughed loudly, I got nervous; was I becoming manic? When my mood was flat, I got twitchy; was I heading for a depression? I monitored myself obsessively, unable to relax and always on alert to something going wrong with my brain. I tried to control the way I felt, to make sure I didn't fall into emotional extremes, but it was hard work and there was no guarantee I could keep extreme emotions at bay. Suppressing joy and pushing away sadness didn't create a harmonious emotional life. It created more stress. I had hoped that with willpower alone, I could somehow resist bipolar's advance, but if the silent assassin decided to strike, there was nothing I could do. This quiet internal war with my emotions was draining and it had now been over two years since I had enjoyed being alive. Bipolar was winning and I was fed up.

"I think you should consider taking lithium," Dr. Wrate suggested. He could see that university had been good for me in a variety of ways, but I needed further support. His words struck a chord. Psychiatric medication is rarely pretty and my experience with Haloperidol had left a dent in my psyche, but I trusted Dr. Wrate and was bright enough to know he was the one person who could get me out of this mess. There were times in my life when I instinctively knew what was the right thing to do. Whether it appeared logical or not, I just knew. This was one of those times.

"Yes, I think I'm ready for that," I replied, feeling a sense of relief as I accepted his idea. I needed help and I was ready to do whatever it took to be myself again.

Lithium Carbonate is a salt and is considered to be one of the most effective medications for treating bipolar. [10] It was first used to treat mania in the nineteenth century and has been used clinically for over seventy years. [11] It is considered to be particularly effective for those who have inherited the disease. In order to work properly, the concentration of lithium has to be at a certain level in the blood. Not too high and not too low. If the level is too high, I could experience vomiting, diarrhea, brain damage, renal toxicity and in the worst case, death. If it is too low, the therapeutic effects diminish and I could become manic, psychotic or depressed. The therapeutic range for lithium is fairly narrow so I would need to have blood tests every three to six months, to make sure I wasn't poisoning myself, but was getting the chemical support I needed.

"Lithium isn't a cure for bipolar, but if it works, it can control your symptoms," Dr. Wrate told me. He warned me there was a risk of long term thyroid and kidney damage, but as a nineteen-year-old, I wasn't too worried about that. Long term damage didn't mean a great deal when I had been alive for less than two decades. For a long time, Dr. Wrate had suspected I might need to take lithium, but he had waited a year before suggesting the drug. He had three reasons for doing so:

Firstly, it was possible I might do well without psychiatric medication, but we needed time to find out.

Secondly, once I began taking lithium, I would probably need it for the remainder of my life because if I stopped, I could become very ill indeed. [12] Finding out for myself, rather than being pushed into long term lithium use, made it more likely I would stick with lithium if I decided to take it.

Thirdly, lithium is unique in that I might only get one shot at it. If I took lithium for a while and then stopped, it couldn't be guaranteed to work again.

It seemed lithium might do a better job of managing my mental health than I had been doing, and may take some of the pressure off me. By trial, error and blood tests, we found a dose which kept me in the therapeutic range and I was good to go.

Dr. Wrate didn't rush my diagnosis and stuff me full of pharmaceuticals as quickly as he could, as sometimes happens in psychiatry. He was considered in his approach, taking time to get to know me, whilst looking at the bigger picture and what would work best for me in the long run. He saw not merely a chemical imbalance, but a young man with spirit who needed to go out and experience the world. He strengthened, rather than scared me; giving me advice on how to stay well, but encouraged me to get out there and live my life. Had he been fearful or overprotective, I might have believed I was fragile and should be wrapped up in cotton wool. By choosing to empower me, rather than making me feel like a victim, he made sure I continued to say "yes" to life rather than "no." I ended up believing I was as capable as any of my friends and have lived a life which hasn't been crippled by fear.

By waiting until I was ready to go on lithium, rather than pressuring me into it, Dr. Wrate opened the doorway for me to take the drug for years and to benefit from it. Had I started to take lithium too early, I would have wondered if I needed it and the chances of me stopping, or not taking it as prescribed, would have been higher. I was now in a place where I was ready to commit to taking lithium carbonate every day for the rest of my days.

Learnings:

1. Having a kind, competent and perceptive psychiatrist was a bonus. My faith in Dr. Wrate made it simple for me to be honest with him and speeded my recovery.

2. My tolerance to stress was greatly reduced after my first episode.

3. It was draining to self-monitor my moods, as I could never truly relax and be myself.

4. Much of the stress I experienced was caused by my mental state and how I interpreted events, rather than the events themselves.

5. It was helpful to have the opportunity to live without medication; it gave me a better understanding of my condition.

6. It was wise for Dr. Wrate to give me time to make up my own mind about taking lithium. This meant that when I decided to, I could do so wholeheartedly.

7. When I was struggling, it was normal for me to push myself to keep going, unaware I needed help. Whenever I got help, it helped.

Chapter 4. Hypomania

"Lithium is feared for its power to take away feeling. All feeling.
Making you into a kind of zombie."

– Stephen Fry, Comedian.

In the winter of 1995, I started taking 1,000 milligrammes of lithium a day and had some significant reactions to the drug. For the whole of the next term at university, I was so sedated I slept for about fourteen hours a night. I stopped paying attention to basic standards of hygiene, such as cleaning my room or washing myself and I lived on a far from nutritious diet of chicken Kievs and chips. I gained three stones in weight and because lithium is a salt, I was thirsty most of the time. My concentration span and memory were affected. I couldn't write intelligible essays, read my textbooks, or even follow what was said in the few lectures I bothered to turn up to. What's more, lithium doped me so profoundly, I never questioned any of these side effects. In fact, I found feeling dopey quite pleasant, so I didn't question that either. As long as I turned up to a few lectures, I could do whatever I liked, which was to sloth around my student flat, eating junk food, sleeping and living like an unruly teenager. Psychiatric medication doesn't solely affect the brain, it affects every part of life because we interact with the world through our brain. If the brain is working well, all areas of life respond to this and if the brain is hindered, all of life responds to that.

Fortunately, after three months, my body acclimatised to lithium and the dopey feeling lifted. I slept for a slightly less slothful ten hours a night and my zest for life returned, although I continued to stuff myself full of chicken Kievs at every available opportunity. That was a habit which would take many years to break. Now my body was used to lithium, I began to reap the full benefits of taking it. The two and a half, chalky-white pills I took every evening, strengthened my wobbly brain, transforming it into a steadier, more resilient version of itself. Extreme highs and lows were barred from my mind and painful emotions could no longer sink their claws into me.

Hurray! Bipolar could no longer wreak havoc in my life!

It was such a boost to feel my brain becoming stronger and the last vestiges of depression evaporate. I felt like an inmate on death row who had been pardoned at the eleventh hour. It was a surprise to me that, despite how traumatic my experiences of depression had been, I no longer feared its return. In fact, I didn't seem to fear anything anymore. Barring a mild nervousness which occasionally fluttered into my mind and a brief spell of panic attacks in my twenties, I felt no fear to speak of for over a decade. Fearlessness is an experience many people would love to have, but in those days a smidgen of well-placed nervousness would have been quite healthy for me. It might have reigned me in and made me think about the consequences of my actions. Instead, I became reckless and began to push the limits as far as I could.

It wasn't only my fear that dried up like a barren creek in the midday sun. I stopped feeling the majority of my emotions; both positive and negative, for long periods of time. Melancholy, sadness, satisfaction, jealousy, love, misery, tenderness, worry and contentment all but disappeared, except on the rare occasions when I had forgotten to take my nightly dose of lithium and its dampening effect wore off. There were two or three times in the next fifteen years, when the emotional pressure built up to such a degree that I felt it. When I was madly in love or heart-broken, lithium's dam was breached and love or sadness found their way into my awareness, but most of the time I felt no emotion at all.

Unless you have taken it yourself, the effect of a mood stabiliser is hard to imagine. What is both interesting and difficult to get a handle on, is that my emotions were still there, but for long periods of time I couldn't feel them. I was numb. Lithium had turned down the volume button on my emotional thermostat, to the degree that I no longer acknowledged their existence. Yet, they did exist. To the outside world I appeared to have a fairly typical emotional life. Emotions still passed through my nervous system and I acted on them, but I didn't feel them anymore.

Emotions are chemical reactions in the brain, triggered by events in our lives. I believe these chemical reactions were happening inside me as they had done before lithium, but now my brain was numbed to them. Imagine you have been injected with a local anesthetic in your leg and then you injure it. Your body goes through the same reactions it would without anesthetic, it bleeds or bruises, but you don't feel the pain. This was similar to what happened to my feelings. The emotions were there, as were the emotional reactions, but the sensation of the feelings went unnoticed. When I got some bad news, I reacted with signs of sadness. If a handsome guy was chatting up my girlfriend, I looked like I was jealous. Yet I didn't feel a thing, I merely reacted to the situation. I remember having a conversation with a couple of university friends about a girl I liked.

"That's crazy. I don't believe it for a second," I snarled aggressively.

"Why are you angry?" One of them asked, a little taken aback.

"I'm not bloody angry," I shouted angrily, but inside I felt neutral. My body language, tone of voice and facial expression, all indicated I was furious and I might well have been, but I didn't feel it.

Looking and acting incongruently with how I felt complicated my relationships, particularly because I had no idea this was happening. I became difficult to read and notoriously unpredictable. My friends and family couldn't understand that I could express emotions, but at the same time was unable to feel them. Although to be fair, why would they? I didn't understand what was going on myself.

My disconnection had drawbacks. Before lithium, if I upset someone, I would feel guilty and usually apologise to them. Once I was on lithium, I no longer felt any guilt, so I rarely apologised. As you can imagine, this was not a great recipe for maintaining healthy relationships. As a youngster the ability to relate to other people's suffering had been one of my gifts, but this vanished and with it much of my sensitivity towards others. I became tougher, less tolerant and created more conflict than I had ever done before. Fortunately, I was still able to be friendly and considerate, so I did form good friendships over those years.

Many patients describe feeling "numbed out" by psychiatric medications and this was true for me, but I was still able to experience happiness. However, it was not the steady, cosy emotional happiness I had previously felt as joy in my heart. It was an elevated state I could lose all too easily. I didn't know it, but I had moved into a state of hypomania which felt both magnificent and intolerably restless.

- **Hypomania:** An abnormally revved-up state of mind which affects your mood, thoughts and behaviour. A hypomanic episode commonly manifests with unusual gaiety, excitement, flamboyance or irritability, along with potential secondary characteristics like restlessness, extreme talkativeness, distractibility, hypersexuality, reduced need for sleep and unusual irritability, excitement, hostility, or aggression. [13]

My body started to experience an intensity it had never done before and would shake as if an electric current was passing through it. I sometimes felt this excess energy was going to make me explode. Tremors are one of lithium's side effects, but I didn't put two and two together. This hypomanic state lasted for most of my university career and went undetected because it manifested as an extension of my already "up" personality.

To the outside world I looked uncommonly happy and overexcitable, but my happiness was as fragile as winter's last snowflake. I easily became quick-tempered, irritable and snappy and I couldn't slow down. It was as if an invisible whirlwind was hurling me through life without caring where I landed. From the moment I woke up, I was full on, going at one hundred miles an hour, until I collapsed into bed at night. It must have been hard work for my flat mates.

For the next fifteen years, I had no idea lithium had impacted my emotions in the way it had, or the extent to which my way of relating to the world had changed. Before lithium, much of what I did and said had been driven by my feelings, but now I had to find another way to relate to the world. The solution was to develop a way of relating to people which didn't require feelings. Rather than using both my intellect and emotions to read situations and interact with other people, as I had previously done, I now relied solely upon my intellect. I intellectualised my emotional life rather than feeling it. This was most obvious with my experience of love. The soft, excited, uplifting feeling I had previously called love was all but gone, but rather than live a loveless life, I began to figure love out in my mind. I *decided* who I loved rather than *felt* who I loved. At the time, I was oblivious to my new approach, which happened without my volition, but it worked quite well. I *knew* who I loved, but I no longer *felt* who I loved. I *knew* my parents loved me, so I loved them back, but rather than *feeling* the love between us I *knew* it instead.

It didn't take long for me to forget that the feeling of love had ever existed. If you wear a pair of tinted glasses, which remove the colour green from your spectrum, you get used to a world with no green in it and blue trees don't shock you at all. As with the colour green, I didn't miss what I had forgotten. Hints of love would occasionally pay me a visit, like passing butterflies on a summer's day, but I rarely felt the full emotional force of love I had felt before I went on lithium.

Many lithium users speak of the challenge of no longer feeling their emotions. They feel that without them, they are no longer themselves. Looking back, the emotional change from pre-lithium to lithium was dramatic, but I didn't really notice my feelings were gone because I quickly moved into hypomania. Had I not become hypomanic, I might have been concerned by the desert which my emotional life had become, but I was young and this new inner state became my new normal.

One of the biggest practical disadvantages of taking lithium was losing my ability to judge situations and make good decisions. We all have a feelings compass, which helps us to navigate our way through this world, but mine had been dismantled. Like a lost sailor, I was cast adrift in the ocean of life, without a sextant to keep me away from the perilous rocks which lined the shore. The hypomania made me more foolish and impetuous. I became thoughtless and numb to the signals ordinary people pick up on. When my best friend died, I didn't feel sad or even bother going to his funeral. I had lived and laughed with him for four years, but I found myself putting his death behind me without a second's thought. The emotions which would have pulled me to his funeral or catalysed my grieving process, simply didn't appear.

In reality, I didn't put his death behind me because I didn't get the chance to mourn him. On various occasions since then I have regretted this fact, wishing I had acted differently and gone to his funeral. I wish I had been in touch with my feelings when he died, then I could have grieved for him and said a proper goodbye.

On a positive note, taking lithium allowed me to stop over-monitoring my moods and I began to relish the freedom of not having to manage bipolar by myself. This was a big deal. I no longer worried about what was going on in my head. Lithium would take care of it. A new life opened up ahead of me, one in which I could trust my mental health and didn't need me to look over my shoulder all the time. I returned to university without fearing I might dive into the depths of despair, and I went on holidays without worrying about getting ill and ending up in a nightmarish psychiatric hospital in a third world country. My inner stability had been returned to me and it was truly a gift to be celebrated.

The subtler ways in which I had experienced pleasure before lithium were now useless to me because I could no longer feel their emotional benefits. I had loved the peace of reading books, but this feeling was gone. I had savoured the satisfaction of cooking good food, but this feeling was gone too. Even walking in nature, which I had enjoyed, was boring and one-dimensional. So I found other ways to enjoy life, through pleasure and entertainment. Fun became my most valuable currency because it gave me a taste of both. I couldn't *feel* alive, but I could *be* alive. I spent my days chasing fun like a man possessed; playing practical jokes, pushing the boundaries and doing anything I could to create more fun. Anything which was wild or outrageous enough to distract me from my violent mind would do. My new demeanour made me both more popular and unpopular than I had ever been.

My days became a confusing concoction of intense, happy, adventurous, argumentative and mildly insane. I was far from normal; throwing axes into doors, writing graffiti on walls, starting arguments, picking fights and antagonising anyone who got on my bad side. With this new intensity, I had both the energy and the lack of inhibitions to live life in excess. I partied, I chased women, I drank, I ran marathons, I fell for women, I played sport, I laughed, I had some success with women and I never stopped doing and doing and doing. The life I lived was exciting, outrageous, hedonistic and as far as I was concerned, truly impressive. I didn't have many inhibitions to start with, but the hypomania made short work of what remained of them. I stripped naked in public, I had sex on trains, I wore ridiculously outlandish clothes, I exuded overconfidence and was rude to people I barely knew. In short, I was larger than life, unconcerned about walking into the university library topless on a freezing autumn day, or breaking into my neighbour's flat to take the fuse out of his rather loud stereo.

It is apparent I would have benefitted from finding a balanced lifestyle. Somewhere between my wild excesses and wrapping myself up in cotton wool. Unfortunately, the middle way was unknown territory to me. I was twenty, consumed by the excitement of university and absorbed by the excesses of a rampant hypomania that everyone thought was me.

I have asked myself, could this drawn-out hypomania have been avoided? If I had learned about bipolar and adopted sensible boundaries to support my mental health, would it have helped? It might have done, but frankly, I don't think I was in a place where I even cared about my health. Dr. Wrate had given me plenty of good advice, but in the haze of hypomania I forgot it and any hint of responsibility disappeared like a thief in the night. Why would I be interested in managing the illness? I was far too busy living at warp speed.

Learnings:

1. When I first started taking lithium my body needed time to adjust.

2. Lithium did a good job of preventing me from becoming manic, depressed or psychotic, but I still developed hypomania. It also stopped me over-monitoring my moods, which took a great deal of pressure off me.

3. On lithium I became restless, my emotions were numbed and my ability to make good choices impaired.

4. I began to intellectualise my relationships rather than feel them. Although I looked like I had emotions, I didn't feel them as I had before.

5. Hypomania was not easy to detect because it exaggerated my existing "up" personality traits. This is the main reason why my first hypomanic episode went undetected for such a long time.

Chapter 5. What is it like to be manic?

"When you are mad, mad like this, you don't know it. Reality is what you see. When what you see shifts, departing from anyone else's reality, it's still reality to you."

– Marya Hornbacher, Madness: A Bipolar Life.

It is nearly impossible to imagine a state of consciousness you have not experienced for yourself. You can read the most beautiful love stories, but until your heart has missed a beat when hearing the footfalls of a lover, you don't know what it is like to be in love.

Having said this, I will do my best to give an insight into how I experience the various states of mania, psychosis and depression.

My manias manifest either as heaven sent, supremely pleasurable euphorias, or as terrifying inner battles that rip my sanity to pieces. I have split them up into four categories based on the symptoms I experience.

1. Euphoric mania: As the name suggests, a euphoric mania feels wonderful beyond words. Being enveloped by this divine state makes me feel blissfully happy, profoundly overconfident and irresponsibly fearless. As high as a kite, I float through life on cloud nine without a care in the world. I still feel like me, but an immeasurably improved version of me, as if my ego has been injected with steroids. I feel sexy, powerful and in the flow. Experiencing a euphoric mania is an astonishing feeling. Creativity flows in ways that are so supported by life it seems anything is possible and within reach.

As a love affair develops with my fertile mind, my ideas become sacred to me and seem to be cocooned in genius. I follow each brilliant idea, until it takes me to another even more appealing one and then I follow that. This makes it challenging for others to follow me in conversation, yet I believe I'm making perfect sense.

Incredible insights find their way into my consciousness, which isn't surprising because God has chosen me to share my brilliance with the world. In a series of intuitive flashes, I understand the complexities of the Cosmos and the answers to questions which have confounded the greatest minds for centuries. The solutions to violence, poverty and world hunger are obvious to me, if only the foolish mortals of earth could understand my message. I possess a complete understanding of the history of humanity and of what lies ahead for the people of this planet. When trying to explain my insights, I become tongue-tied and incapable of verbalising my genius. I resort to scribbling rough diagrams on scraps of toilet paper, but still, no one understands. How can they?

Life adopts a magical quality with me as the magician at the centre of it all. Each day is an adventure. It is alive, exciting and filled with synchronicities. I consistently get a good parking spot, or my favourite table in a busy restaurant and the waitresses love me. Who wouldn't? If I think of a song, the next shop I walk into will be playing it. Feelings of confidence, dynamism, well-being and allure ooze from every pore in my body and I radiate a mania-charged magnetism.

My heightened energy and enthusiasm draw people towards me as if they are under a hypnotic spell. At parties, everyone crowds around me, hanging on my every word and every joke I tell. I spend a great deal of my time on the hunt, flirting or chatting up the opposite sex, feeding my ego with their attention. I am convinced I can do the impossible. So forceful with my ideas, that it is challenging for my friends to do anything other than go along with them. I draw them into my outlandish theories and they play along nervously, their words of reason unable to touch my deluded fantasies. I was once certain I would never age, believing meditation would keep my body young indefinitely. I tried to explain to my wife why my DNA was unique and she ended up agreeing with me; although I suspect this was only to get me to leave her alone.

In a euphoric mania I believe I will succeed in whatever task I do. It doesn't make a difference how outlandish or unrealistic it is. Whether it be becoming the best stockbroker in the world, writing a New York Times best seller or saving humanity from the brink of environmental disaster, I can do it. Had I not been confined to a hospital bed during one of my worst manias, I would probably have spent all my money on ridiculous projects and bankrupted myself.

In this state I show an arrogant disinterest in other people's opinions. What do they know? I have access to secret knowledge they can never understand. I sometimes talk like a megalomaniac and had I been in a position of power during my manias, I think I would have abused it terribly.

Having said this, the discoveries I have made during some manias, illustrate the overlap which can occur between madness, reality and spiritual states. One of the strangest elements of mania is that it gives me understandings which are far beyond what I experience when well. I can understand why mania is sometimes described as spiritual, because it expands my mind beyond the confines of everyday thinking and opens up other ways of experiencing reality.

When manic, I sometimes find myself connected to what seem like exaggerated spiritual states, but these states are not grounded in the stability that comes from a true spiritual practice. They are more like larger-than-life hallucinations, combined with cosmic insights and discoveries. A truly spiritual state is based in presence and inner quiet, rather than chaotic, dreamlike scenarios. It is grounded and in touch with reality.

Although my manias are ungrounded and confusing, I have learned secrets about the cosmos and my place in the universe, that I never thought I would know. Truths, that I eventually had confirmed after years of meditation and spiritual work, were revealed to me in those highs. It is no surprise that a state of insanity, which can lead to fantastic feats of creativity, is somehow connected to a higher power.

Lying in a hospital bed, I once perceived that there was only one permanent thing in the whole universe; a field of presence or consciousness which had no limits or boundaries. This field could not be seen; but everything I saw, felt, smelled, touched or tasted existed within it. It united everything with its presence. Through years of spiritual work, I later discovered my insight was true, but this time, my discovery came from a peaceful state of consciousness, not a crazy high. It was an experienced reality rather than a clever idea.

When manic, I have times when I become psychic. Some mornings I think of five people and all of them contact me that day. I can read people like open books and know things about their past only they know. It is remarkable. The mind seems to have a far greater capacity than I ever imagined and some of this capacity is unlocked by mania. I would happily spend the rest of my days in this close to perfect experience, but it never lasts for more than a couple of weeks. If left untreated, the euphoria develops into a far uglier, agitated mania that is equally out of control.

2. Agitated mania: Imagine it is Monday morning. It is cold, pouring with rain and you're on your way out of the front door carrying too many things. You've had a bad night's sleep and are buzzing from the three cups of coffee you've already knocked back today. You're late for a vital business meeting, have had a fight with your partner and your most demanding client is ringing you on your mobile phone right now. You look back and see your partner rushing after you in tears, but you haven't got time to talk. So, you ignore them and rush to get on the bus before they manage to catch up with you. Once you have pushed your way onto the crowded bus, you soon discover you've left your briefcase in your car, which is parked on the other side of town.

"Noooooo," you shout, realising you have lost your company its biggest contract. Your mind is going crazy, you're confused and very agitated.

The early stages of an agitated mania feel similar to this and then it gets worse. My thoughts, speech and actions quicken and I become unpredictable, paranoid and unreasonable. I can't stop talking and often explode over the most minor details. I say cruel things without caring they are cruel and dominate conversations, uninterested in what anyone else has to say. After all, I am right and they are stupid. My voice becomes strident and my eyes dangerous, burning threateningly as if they are on fire. I have an air of violence about me, which makes other people nervous. Typical societal inhibitions vanish as I strip naked in public to make my friends laugh. Then, for no reason, I retreat into myself and worry about the state of the world. In agitated manias, fear is close at hand, along with dystopic thoughts and fantasies.

The slow pace of everyday life is intolerable to me. I jump from topic to topic and get frustrated with those who are understandably confused. When my friends show concern, I get angry with them too. I *have* to keep moving, getting up, walking around, sitting down, getting back up again. I have to keep pushing on, my relentless mind driving me forward at a rate of knots. It is exhausting for me and for everyone around me. I lose my sense of self-control, ruled by the pinball insanity bouncing around my head.

In my case, an agitated mania sometimes follows a euphoric mania and sometimes develops on its own. If I was euphoric before it develops, the people I had previously drawn to me are now repelled by the chaotic, aggressive, high-speed chatter tumbling from my mouth. Curiously, mania suppresses the mechanisms in my mind which tell me I am too tired, too weak or I can't do something. This means I become physically stronger, able to run faster and lift heavier weights, because my mind no longer holds my body back.

Apart from medication, nothing I know can fully calm my euphoric or agitated manias once they have begun in earnest. Getting enough sleep helps, but sleep doesn't come easily in this state.

3. Simultaneous mania and depression: This is the most emotionally confusing and unstable state that I have experienced. Unstable, because neither mania nor depression dominates and the two often mix with each other. My mind is racing, but also consumed with feelings of depression, fear and agitation.

I usually move from a low to a high over the course of the day. My mornings are depressed and then agitation and fear increase as the day goes on. By the time the evening comes, my depression has been replaced with an ungrounded and agitated high. It is both physically and mentally tiring to be dragged from bliss to despair and then back again, day after day. In this state I find it almost impossible to sleep without medication to help me.

4. Hypomania (see Chapter 4 and pages 131 and 163).

My first manic episode took me by surprise because I had never experienced anything like it before. So, I had no context in which to understand what was happening to me. It was my final year of school and the possibility I was becoming mentally ill could not have been further from my mind. I had a very loud and highly-strung personality, so no one, including myself, took much notice when I became gradually more so. I can't be sure what catalysed that first mania, but in the nineties, genetics were regarded to be the main cause of bipolar. Nowadays, evidence suggests that childhood trauma can also play a significant role. [14] Whether it was my genes, exam stress, hormonal changes, a traumatic birth, or something else which pushed me over the edge, I will probably never know. Either way, I think it is likely it was only a matter of time before something awakened this sleeping monster and gave it the chance to gnash its voracious teeth.

Looking back at myself as a child, it is clear I was at risk of developing mental problems later in life. I had a nervous temperament and was a perfectionist. I put myself under enormous pressure to be good at things, rather than appreciating them for their own sake. I had an up and down personality; one minute enthusiastic and happy, anxious and worried the next. Recurrent nightmares plagued me and my thoughts were often harsh and violent.

When I was eleven, all of the pupils in my class were pitted against each other in an academic league table. At the end of each term, a sheet with all of our names and our final position, was pinned to the school notice board for all to see. I always came top of my class and revelled in the positive attention this attracted. I had one rival; a studious girl called Amy. Amy had a razor-sharp mind and shared my fanatical desire to come top of the class, but thus far I had managed to fend her off. Then disaster struck. The day before my exams, I broke my collarbone and was told to take a few days off school. I hit the roof. If Amy beat me, I couldn't take it. I was not going to let her steal my rightful place as number one.

Although my collar bone ached and I could hardly hold a pen, I tried to persuade my parents to take me to school to sit my exams. Even with a broken clavicle, I knew I could beat Amy. My parents, being good parents, refused. All the other children would have jumped at the chance to miss those exams, but I couldn't bear the thought of it. Whether these neurotic traits were a symptom of bipolar or ended up causing the condition, I can't be sure, but I know stress builds on itself, which means a tendency to get stressed leads to more of the same.

Some bipolar sufferers do not experience an equal number of manias and depressions, having a propensity for one or other of the two poles. The majority spend more time depressed than manic. [15] As an enthusiastic extrovert who liked getting stuck into life, my tendency was to become manic. Had I been the melancholic type, perhaps depression would have been the pole towards which I graduated.

With every manic episode I have had, the mania developed gradually, creeping its way into my mind over weeks rather than days. This insidious assault initially made a developing mania hard to spot. The difference between having a few great days and the start of a euphoric mania wasn't easy to recognise. In the beginning of a euphoric mania, I would feel so good I had no reason or inclination to suspect that anything was amiss.

Thirty years and many manias later, I am now well equipped to spot the early warning signs of an episode. Thanks primarily to the skills I have developed through meditation, I have learned to be aware of what my mind is up to and can observe my thoughts rather than be consumed by them. When I observe my thoughts, I am like a lighthouse keeper standing next to a bright, illuminating beam. If bad weather is approaching or a ship is in trouble, I can see it from a distance.

With each manic episode, I have learned more about the warning signs. I have also learned to listen to my family and friends when they are worried about me. They are good at spotting the signs, but it is usually me who notices them first. Observing is one of the most important skills I have learned because it gives me time to address a mania before I lose myself in it. Addressing a mania, invariably means taking antipsychotic medication, which stabilises my mind. I keep a box of antipsychotics close at hand; in case any symptoms like fear, rushing thoughts or euphoria appear. This gives me considerable peace of mind and allows me to live a freer life.

Learnings:

1. Through meditation (see Chapter 15) I have learned to observe my thoughts, which makes it easier to spot the early signs which precede an episode (see Chapter 7).

2. Every mania I experience makes it easier to catch the next one.

3. My ability to spot the early warning signs brings me peace of mind. Although I can become ill at any time, I have the medication to treat it simply and effectively, as long as I notice it is happening.

Chapter 6. What is it like to be depressed?

"If you're that depressed, reach out to someone. And remember, suicide is a permanent solution, to a temporary problem."

– Robin Williams, Comedian.

When I was first diagnosed with bipolar, I was told it was caused by a chemical imbalance in my brain. This imbalance then manifested as a sickness which overtook my mind. The brain and the mind are distinct and separate entities. The brain is a physical structure found between our ears which "integrates sensory information and directs motor responses." [16] It acts as a control centre; by receiving, interpreting and directing sensory information throughout the body. The mind has no physical structure. It is a collection of thoughts, feelings and emotions and, although it feels like it exists in our head, its exact location is unknown.

Our minds are unique to us; formed through life experiences, circumstances and perhaps genetics too. Some people have positive minds and they tend to be optimistic, accepting and happy. They are often lucky, well-liked and successful in their chosen areas of endeavour. They see the world as a friendly place. Others have minds which are dominated by negativity. Negative minds create pessimistic, judgmental and unhappy people. People who are more likely to be unpopular, attract conflict and misfortune and see the world as a hostile place. Although they may be successful, they don't get to relish their success for long because their negative minds won't allow it. Most of us lie somewhere in the middle ground between these two extremes.

Whatever type of mind we possess, and it can change over time, it is something we learn to live with. We get used to our thoughts and emotions and we get on with life. From as far back as I can remember, my mind fluctuated between positive and negative. This is normal, but every now and again my poles moved further apart. My positive side became ludicrously unrealistic and my negative side, hateful and despairing. I would jump between these poles without warning or reason, sometimes flipping from overexcited to anxious many times a day.

Over the last thirty years, I have experienced about a dozen depressive episodes, which have varied in duration and severity. The shortest was a few days, the longest lasted for nearly a year. Depression is an extreme expression of the negative pole and in its most severe forms can lead to suicide or even starvation from neglect. Before I experienced bipolar, I had never been suicidal, but once the condition revealed itself, suicidal thoughts and desires became a part of my life. By observing what was going on inside my head, I have identified two aspects of my mind which can push me towards suicide. These are suicidal thoughts and suicidal emotions.

Suicidal thoughts are voices or words in my mind, which try to persuade me to take my own life.

"I want to die."

"You'd be better off dead."

"I hate myself."

"You're scum," would be common ones. The voices which speak these thoughts use both the first and second person and sound like me. Suicidal emotions are wordless but feel accursed, nonetheless. You might think that thoughts which tell me to kill myself would be more painful than mere emotions, but they aren't. When I have suicidal emotions, I feel them in my body and my mind, either as a thick, oppressive fog in my head, or as a stagnant heavy knot in my chest. Suicidal thoughts exist solely in my head and have no bodily sensations associated with them. Thoughts tend to appear and disappear quite quickly, whereas emotions like to hang around. If thoughts are like firecrackers, emotions are the smoke that is left behind, lingering in the air as a thick, grey mist. This is not to say loud, repetitive, suicidal thoughts are easy for me to deal with, but they aren't as debilitating as suicidal emotions.

The average person has between 20,000 and 60,000 thoughts passing through their mind every day. Around 90 percent of these are repetitive. [17] If you are someone who has around 60,000 a day, that means you experience roughly one every second and a half. This can be tiring. Unless you have practiced meditation or some other form of awareness training, you have probably not learned to "observe" your thoughts. Unobserved thoughts are dangerous because we don't know they are there. They are incognito, able to twist and manipulate us without our knowledge. This means we unconsciously think them and are hoodwinked into believing whatever they tell us. When we have learned to observe our thoughts, we are no longer controlled by them, we can create a distance which robs them of much of their power to make us suffer. Most people have no distance from their thoughts and believe whatever their fickle mind says without question. That is why unobserved thoughts can be harmful. As most people's thoughts are unobserved, the quality and quantity of our thoughts fundamentally affects our mental health.

How a thought affects me depends on my emotional state. Suicidal thoughts are never pleasant, but when I am in a balanced mood, they don't bother me too much. I can observe them, let them be and after a while they usually disappear. If they persist, I take it as a signal that a depression may be on its way and I contact my doctor. When suicidal thoughts combine with suicidal emotions, they fuel each other and rob me of the ability to observe my thoughts. This means the skills I have developed through meditation are no longer within my reach (Please note that during a manic, depressive or psychotic episode I can't observe my thoughts. Meditation is only helpful when I am well. It is not advisable to meditate when mentally ill or mentally unstable.)

Unlike mania and psychosis, I sometimes receive no warning of an impending depression. It can hit me out of the blue. One day all is well and the next I wake up feeling heavy and hopeless. It isn't only me who feels the depression, the people around me feel it too. Like a lead weight, my depression pulls them downwards; unfortunately, depression can be contagious. I have categorised the depressions I have experience into three groups (It is heartening to note that have not experienced the moderate or severe depressions for over five years, but I sometimes still experience a mild depression which can last two or three days):

1. Mild depression: For me this is like the winter blues. I have a negative outlook on life and feel sad, but not desperate. My sense of humour vanishes, I'm lethargic and I sleep more than usual. I lose interest in the things I usually enjoy such as food, sex, sport, writing or socialising and it is hard to motivate myself to perform mundane tasks. I am able to pick my wife up at the airport, but I can't greet her with a smile. In this state, I struggle to take good care of myself, I shower less and I can't be bothered to cook proper meals. I cry easily, but although my tears are sad, they aren't saturated with sorrow. Knowing I could sink into a deeper depression scares me, but my levels of anxiety are not too high.

I won't feel like it, but if I force myself to be honest about what's going on, I can ask for help. If I explain to my wife how I feel, she is understanding and gives me encouragement. If I speak to a doctor, psychiatrist or psychologist, they are usually able to help. When my wife realises what is going on, she gives me tasks to do, which are helpful. These tasks tend to be simple, but they keep my mind off how I am feeling and stop me from wallowing in self-pity all day. Even though it seems like the most tempting thing for me to do, mulling around the house thinking negative thoughts is not good for me. It is much better that I am active.

Spending time with upbeat people, getting out of the house, watching comedy, exercising or doing something I enjoy can lift me out of this mild depression. Reminders that there is light at the end of the tunnel are valuable too. Although, I have shaken off mild depressions without medication or professional help; but they can easily descend into a deeper one.

2. Moderate depression: Grief and sadness are a normal part of life, but in a moderate depression they became oppressive and couldn't be relieved by talking with friends or having a good cry. In a moderate depression, I had so little energy that getting out of a chair was a huge undertaking, let alone getting out of bed. My past, present and future were black holes and being left alone scared me. Nothing gave me pleasure and I showed scant awareness of my surroundings. Performing simple tasks required a great deal of effort and getting dressed could be so demanding that I didn't bother.

In one of my longer moderate depressions, I couldn't bring myself to change my underwear because my brain couldn't cope with this simple task. I wore the same boxershorts every day for three weeks. I cried for no reason, but my tears were filled with anguish. I was unable to engage with other people and was bombarded by anxiety attacks. Fear was my constant companion, which made me jumpy and reactive. My first reaction to everything was fear or hopelessness. Going to the airport to pick up my wife would have been an impossible task and even the suggestion would have sent me into a spiral of anxiety.

My mind was permanently negative. Convincing me I was worthless, not fit to be a friend, or stepfather, or partner. I saw everything in black and white, as if the mental dexterity to absorb nuances had been removed. My thoughts, which I was no longer able to observe, were monotonous and relentless, giving me no space to think anything positive about myself or the world.

To confound the inescapability of this hopeless state, I couldn't motivate myself to get out of it. The part of my brain that usually pushed me to get well, no longer worked. I could go for a walk (if my wife told me to) or shop for food (if she wrote the list), but more than that was out of the question. If I was in the house alone, I would sit in a chair and suffer.

3. Severe depression: Hell doesn't exist as some far-off place where sinners go when they die. Hell exists between our ears and is created by the thoughts and feelings in our mind. When I experienced severe depression, I was both mentally ravaged and physically debilitated too. Never before had I been broadsided by my feelings in this way. I had experienced fear and anxiety, I had been angry and jealous and sad, but now these simple emotions were magnified a thousand-fold. Depression, fear, panic, guilt and a dark sense of shame smothered me in an excruciating blanket of desperation and self-hatred.

All the flavours of every negative emotion I had ever experienced were bundled into one ghastly sack, thrown over my head and tied tightly around my neck, choking the life out of me. It was a state of endless abandonment and all-encompassing despair. My entire life became an unyielding agony with no hope of relief. The world had no colour, no taste, no smell, no warmth, no love, no friendliness, no hope, no future, no life. It was so bereft of joy, connection and pleasure I would have welcomed death had I been able to imagine it. However, the relief of death was not offered to me. Nothing was offered other than continuous, agonising torment.

There was no way out. This acutely alone state felt permanent, with no prospect of it ever ending. I had no hope of recovery because in this state hope didn't exist. I couldn't even fight, or accept, or strive to get well because I was cut off from life itself. Every task felt undoable, every action a strain. Getting dressed, brushing my teeth or even showering wasn't possible without help. Picking up a fork and putting food into my mouth was like trying to move a small mountain. I remember a nurse putting two pairs of clean socks on the end of my bed and all I could do was stare at them, unable to choose which one to wear. Tears streamed down my face because deciding which socks to wear was too difficult. No words of comfort made any difference to me. I was beyond help, beyond rescue.

Suicidal thoughts were super-glued to the inside of my head and refused to leave. Even if I'd had one positive thought, the negativity of the suicidal ones would have swallowed it up in an instant. Once this state got a grip, it took on a life of its own and I could do nothing to pull myself out of it. My only respite came when I fell asleep, but as soon as I awoke, my head was again dunked into the bucket of suffering and I was left to slowly drown. My inability to do anything gave me a glimpse into why some people end up dying from a severe depression. Not killing themselves, as many do, but actually dying from it. I once met a man who later became severely depressed and ended his days starving to death alone in his own flat, unable to feed himself or pick up the phone and ask for help.

It is important to note that although the care of the hospital staff and my family didn't directly improve my mood, when severely depressed, it helped me to get through it in one piece. In short, it kept me alive. The only way I believe I could ever have recovered from this experience was hospitalisation, the right medication and time. If any of these had been absent, I don't think I would have survived.

Some people try to encourage a depressed person to "pull themself together," but on the rare occasions where anyone tried this approach with me, it didn't work. If I could have pulled myself together, I would have done so. I would have done anything to get out of that state.

Whilst in depression's grip, I could not see anything good about it, but once I recovered, I had enough distance to choose how I viewed the depression. I went through periods of soul searching, where I tried to make sense of what I had been through. I could easily have become bitter and resentful for what I had gone through, but I chose to view it another way.

There is no doubt in my mind that my suffering, though utterly undesirable, has matured me as a person. It has opened my eyes to other people's suffering and given me more empathy and compassion towards them. I could have been that person who grumpily tells a depressed person to "pull themselves together," but because I have been there, I would now meet them with kindness and understanding. Depression showed me how fragile my happiness can be and forced me to re-define my values. It stripped away so many superficial ideas about what is important in life and left a deeper, stronger core of values. Being a good person became more important to me, as did making the world a better place. I also learned the importance of asking for help and being open.

Learnings:

1. Suicidal thoughts and suicidal emotions are different entities.

2. How a suicidal thought affects me depends on my emotional state at the time.

3. When suicidal thoughts and emotions arrived at the same time, they were at their most dangerous.

4. The "pull yourself together" approach did not help me when I was depressed.

5. Depression helped me to grow into a more mature, compassionate and kind person.

6. Depression taught me I can't beat a serious imbalance in brain chemistry with willpower alone. I need to ask for help.

Chapter 7. What is it like to be psychotic?

"Psychosis is when people lose some contact with reality. This might involve seeing or hearing things that other people cannot see or hear (hallucinations) and believing things that are not actually true (delusions)."

– NHS website definition.

Of all the aspects of bipolar type one, psychosis is the state in which I am at my most insane. It is an experience where the illness dances in the depths of my subconscious, creating fictitious scenarios more akin to a bad acid trip than to real life. All of the psychoses I have experienced have been unique, but can be grouped into two main categories; "thought driven" and "total" psychoses.

Thought driven psychoses are characterised by me believing things which are not true. These beliefs create repetitive thoughts (often bizarre and paranoid) and overpowering feelings (usually fear). The world I see remains the same, but what I believe about it changes dramatically.

Total psychoses are also characterised by me believing things which are not true, but on top of this, I see, hear and feel things which aren't there. These visual and audial hallucinations are what truly defines a total psychosis. Entire worlds full of terror, lust, fantasy, fear, conspiracy, adventure, bliss and elation are created in my mind. Worlds I live in and interact with, which seem as real as this one.

The duration of a psychosis usually depends on its severity. The more severe it is, the sooner my loved ones see that I need help. I have lived with minor psychotic symptoms for years without anyone noticing, but once they become serious, I need medication to bring me back to earth.

1. Thought driven psychosis: My mind is overrun by thoughts which tell me stories I would never believe when well. These stories revolve around fear, punishment and impending doom. There are no visual or audial hallucinations; the world I see and hear remains the same, but my beliefs about it are warped. The story of the girl at the swimming pool, whom I feared might accuse me of rape, was a good example of a thought driven psychosis. My fears were not logical, but this didn't stop my overactive mind from churning up streams of paranoid thoughts and fearful feelings. I would wake up in the middle of the night, sweating, terrified of going to prison. My waking moments were viewed through this same paranoia. I was jumpy, hunted and on edge, plagued by a feeling that I had done something terrible and was waiting to be punished for it.

On my first day in the Royal Edinburgh Hospital, I saw the same hospital as the sane people around me saw, but I interpreted it wholly differently. I didn't hallucinate undercover policemen hiding in the wards, but in my mind,

I was sure they were there. The psychosis was so convincing that I wouldn't talk to the doctors or nurses because I believed they were prison guards.

In another thought driven psychosis, I thought that trolls and fairies were living in the woods around my home. What's more, I would go out in the evenings searching for them. Although I never saw a single one, I believed they were there.

To some degree, we all interpret our reality differently to those around us – same reality, different way of seeing it. This is because we experience our lives through the filter of our thoughts and feelings which are unique to us. Life is more subjective than we are led to believe, which means the content of our thoughts and the nature of our feelings hugely impact how we experience life. One person can look at a homeless man begging on the street and see someone who's down on his luck. They might smile at the man and throw some change into his bowl. Another person might glance at the same man on the same street and see a criminal who has thrown his life away. They might put their head down and hurry past, worried he is about to rob them.

Another characteristic of thought driven psychoses is attributing significant meaning to things which have none. The kitchen clock doesn't just tell the time, it passes on clandestine messages from a secret occult society, that has been monitoring me since birth. If I hear people talking in the distance, they aren't shooting the breeze, they are discussing me. In great depth.

Fear dominates my thought driven psychoses, leading to bizarre behaviour. When I believed that I might be executed at any time, I acted strangely indeed. I once thought my wife was a witch who planned to murder me and

I refused to sleep in the same house as her. Having her husband fearing that she was trying to kill him, wasn't easy for her. My paranoia made it harder for doctors and nurses to treat me and keep me safe. Whilst in a mental hospital in Australia, I kept running away from the nurses because I was convinced they were hit men. I can't imagine this improved the quality of care that I received.

I had some fascinating experiences, which showed me the boundaries between reality and unreality are not as defined as I would previously have believed. This became apparent when going for a walk with my wife whilst in a state of mild psychosis. We came to a busy road and as a grey car drove past, I could hear what sounded like demonic chattering coming from inside the vehicle. My wife heard nothing. When the car was a hundred metres up the road, a deer emerged from the woods and bounded in front of it. The car hit it square on. Instead of stopping, the car accelerated away, leaving the wounded animal lying alone on the road. I ran to the stricken deer and kneeling next to her, I placed my hand on her chest, whispering gently.

A minute or two later, I felt her heart slow and then stop. The psychic sense that had been activated by my psychosis had been correct, the people in the grey car were not good people and proved this by leaving an injured animal to die in the road.

2. Total psychosis: My early psychoses were all thought-based, but as the years have gone by, they have developed into total psychoses. A total psychosis not only alters what I believe, but what I see, hear, touch and smell too. The hallucinations mean I don't merely interpret the world differently, I see entirely different worlds.

For me, the beginning of a total psychosis is characterised by fear. It isn't a sporadic fear that pops up from time to time, but an ongoing, underlying anxiety. Then I begin to catch sight of objects in the corner of my eye that aren't there. I might catch sight of a bird flying past, but think it is a person throwing a rock at my head. As the psychosis continues, I develop full-blown hallucinations; people's eyes shine brightly, their skin becomes green and their friendly smiles strike fear into my heart. My mind becomes dominated by thoughts of vampires or werewolves and the appearance of the world itself begins to change before my eyes. A day or two later, people transform into evil reptiles right in front of me.

I once walked into a café and had a conversation with two ghosts who lived there. One was a disfigured pirate with a peg leg and a gruesome, pink scar across his throat. The other was a half-bird, half-man, who moved unimaginably slowly because he was hundreds of years old. They were both dead, but they didn't know it. Neither of them existed, but I didn't know it.

Psychotic worlds don't obey the rules of natural law. Anything can happen inside them. I once experienced life as a half-starved Special Forces sniper in Vietnam, who had been held captive in a bamboo hut for months on end. I felt hunger in my stomach and the heat of the jungle on my skin, but in reality I was in Oslo in the middle of winter. I then jumped into a life as an inmate in a futuristic prison. My wrists were manacled in front of me with electric handcuffs, so I wandered around my flat unable to pull my hands apart. My wife cottoned onto what was happening and unlocked my handcuffs with an imaginary key. It worked! I was able to use my hands again.

In all of my psychoses I was the centre of attention, usually in an exaggerated and self-important way. I might be a powerful politician who was significant to the future of our planet, or a martyr whose suffering was of paramount importance to the people of earth. My psychotic delusions are far from humble!

I remember once being Cinderella, standing by the sink in our kitchen doing the washing up, whilst drifting in and out of a magical realm. The room around me sparkled with lights and legions of talking mice scurried around my bare feet. Held captive in a magical castle, after an evil king had kidnapped me, I heard a noise. I froze, fearing it was the dungeon master coming to beat me. Holding a dirty plate and washing up brush, I stood stock still, not moving an inch, the water still running from the tap. If I didn't move, he wouldn't see me. The things I did to get out of washing the dishes!

Another time, I fell out of bed at two o'clock in the morning and lay on the floor staring at the ceiling unable to move. I had a faraway look in my eyes, as if the lights were on but nobody was at home. My anxious wife pleaded with me to come back, but I didn't respond. She began to panic, worried that I was lost in madness and might never return. I, on the other hand, had teleported light years away, to a far-flung region of outer space, where I was cocooned in a bubble of peace by guardians who had vowed to keep me safe.

As each psychosis deepened, the worlds became more malleable, sometimes even responding to my thoughts, desires and fears. If I thought of Scotland; bagpipe playing soldiers would come marching over a hill and thistles would sprout up around me. If I sensed magic in the air; I might look up at the sky and see an enormous, winged, fire-breathing dragon, twice the size of a Jumbo jet, gliding through the clouds. The world responded to my thoughts!

A psychotic episode is not the same as having an overactive imagination. As a child I would sit on the bough of a tree in our garden, imagining I was a heroic knight and the bough was my trusty steed. I wanted my horse to come to life, but when push came to shove, I knew I was just a boy up a tree. If the same desire had emerged when I was in a total psychosis, I might have found myself in a new world; feeling the wind on my face and the pounding of the horse's hooves beneath me, as I charged into battle. An entire world would be created by my desire, a world which I could touch and see as clearly as you can see the words on this page.

On another occasion, I was a street fighter who had lost a bare-knuckle fist fight. Sitting in a café with my wife, I nursed a black eye that stung and a broken arm that ached. In reality I wasn't hurt at all, but I felt the pain of both injuries as if they were real. I secretly gestured to a man sitting on another table, signalling to him that a drug deal was going down. He responded by looking away and sipping his coffee deliberately slowly, a coded signal that the deal was on. As my wife and I walked home, I scowled at passersby, who backed away nervously, after all I was a street fighter. To this day, I have no idea if they did indeed back away, or if the whole thing was made up in my head. Whilst all this was happening, my wife had no idea I was in psychosis because I didn't dare to talk about what was going on.

My secrecy came from two factors. One was the fact that I was too absorbed in the psychosis to know I was psychotic. The idea of raising the alarm didn't occur to me. The other was that in the beginning of most of my psychoses,

I was taken to some strange dimension and sworn to secrecy. I had to swear an oath of allegiance; or promise someone I loved that I would keep my mouth shut no matter what. This caused me a lot of problems because I didn't dare to ask for help when I needed to.

For a decade, I experienced visual hallucinations every day, but I didn't slip into a full-blown psychosis. During this time, I managed to hold down a part time job and live a fairly normal life. Surprisingly, I had no idea I was hallucinating because the hallucinations had crept up on me so slowly they seemed to be an ordinary part of life. I also had audial hallucinations, where all sound disappeared and I couldn't hear anything: not the wind, the sea or even the ringing of my phone. Years later, I was astonished to learn that hallucinations are listed as one of lithium's side effects.

There were two years in my late thirties when I stopped taking lithium, which led to my most intense total psychoses. I began "jumping" into other worlds. One moment I would be walking in a park, and the next a pack of ravenous dogs would be pursuing me through an unknown city. Before the dogs caught me, I jumped back to safety in the park.

At the beginning of a psychosis, I would jump to another world for a few minutes and then jump back into real life for a few hours. Yet as the psychosis developed my stay in this other world extended to minutes, then hours and finally days. The times when I returned were particularly tough for my wife because she thought the psychosis was over, only for me to be dragged back into it. I knew when this was happening and fought to stay away from those horrible worlds, but it was too much for me. In the end the psychosis invariably won. I hated myself for succumbing to it.

In the early nineties, a television series called *Quantum Leap*, told the story of a physicist, Sam Beckett, who took part in a time travel experiment which went wrong. Every week Sam would leap through time and find himself in someone's body at various times in history, trying to correct their mistakes. Once he fixed the mistake, he jumped somewhere else, always hoping it would be his final jump home, but it never was. Like Sam, I too jumped into a variety of worlds. As the psychosis gained momentum, my trips to these other realms lasted longer, until they became my reality. As I became progressively manic, the speed and number of jumps accelerated. I began to jump between realities so fast that I could experience the joy of a newborn, the agony of a soldier shot to pieces by a sniper and the ecstasy of making love to an angel, all in a matter of seconds.

At one point, I was experiencing about thirty different realities a day, flipping between them every few seconds like a slideshow. I was a client in an Asian massage parlor, I was raped by four friends and I was executed. Every part of my body and face was slowly shot to pieces by a hidden assassin, I lived with a Chinese heroin addict and was an honoured guest in a celestial pleasure house. I lived as an undead yogi in a cave after my own death, flew a spaceship through the cosmos and was a polar explorer. I was the most dangerous prisoner in the world and then a man who drowned in a chemical spill with rats swimming into my mouth. I was a porn star and a superhero hamster, who transformed into a flying rodent. I also experienced my own birth and vampire attacks. These scenarios may sound like plots from some sketchy, low-budget movies, but they were absolutely real to me. I could feel everything that happened to me; every cut, slash, bullet wound or bite. I believe these nightmarish scenarios came from my subconscious because they so often related to fears, desires, or experiences from my past. The human brain isn't designed to be put under the enormous pressure these experiences create and it took me over three years to recover.

The body and mind are intimately connected, which meant that my physical appearance changed depending on which realm I was in. As a newborn, my face was a picture of peace and glee, but as a soldier I looked pale and gaunt. The changes were so stark that my wife could sometimes tell which dimension I was in, merely by looking at my face.

One psychotic realm was unique because I only entered it when I heard the song *Demons* by the group *Imagine Dragons*. I called this realm the dragon realm and it was both scary and intriguing at the same time. Whenever my favourite song played, I began to sob uncontrollably and a dark-green mist enveloped everything around me. I felt myself being dragged into another realm and haunting music replaced the original song. Flaming torches appeared on the walls and I morphed into a flesh-eating reptile. Finally, descending into this dark realm to join my dragon kin for feasts and orgies. What was particularly strange about this place was that it felt so familiar, as if I had been there before in another existence. At some time in my distant past, it had been my home.

Not all the realms I visited were full of demons; some were heavenly; homes to angels, goddesses, mythical creatures, the Knights of the Grail and the Maidens of Avalon. They were saturated in golden light and had green pastures and lush, rich woodlands that stretched as far as the eye could see. Some were ethereal in nature, made entirely out of light. Whilst others were impossible to describe. I felt them, rather than saw them with my own eyes. When experiencing these realms, I was filled with bliss and peace. They provided a much-needed rest from the darker worlds and had I been able to, I would have stayed in these wonderful places forever. Their light, warmth and love were more tantalising than anything I have ever experienced on earth. I wish I could write more about these marvelous places, but for some reason I can only remember the monstrous worlds in great detail.

Spring and autumn are the times of year when psychotic symptoms are most likely to appear in my mind. There seem to be many triggers that can set them off, such as a very bad night's sleep, travelling, chiropractic adjustments, deep massage, intense exercise, taking certain supplements or even herbal remedies. Much of my vulnerability depends on how long it has been since my last psychosis. The more recent the psychosis, the easier it is for my brain to slip into another one. My theory regarding this, is that the neuronal pathways which facilitated a previous psychosis have been stimulated during it. This means that it is easier for my brain to take those pathways again, if they are once more stimulated. The good news is that the longer I go without a psychosis the more likely I will avoid another.

Learnings:

1. I experienced two main types of psychosis: thought based and total. Total psychoses were the most extreme and involved hallucinations, including jumping to other worlds.

2. When I was deep in a psychosis, I was not aware of it because I was lost in the experience itself.

3. I usually didn't talk about being in psychosis, either because I had been sworn to secrecy in some mysterious realm or I was too absorbed in the psychosis to be that self-

aware.

4. My physical appearance changed depending on which mind-created realm I was living in.

5. The longer I stay healthy after a psychosis, the less likely it is to strike again. I can build up resilience to psychoses by looking after myself and avoiding triggers.

Chapter 8. In between episodes

"Adversity introduces you to you."

– Albert Einstein.

When emerging from an episode, one of the biggest challenges I face is coming to terms with the devastation left in its wake. It feels like looking back on the path of a tornado which has smashed its way through the small town called "Oliver." My world has been uprooted, sucked into the eye of the storm, ripped to pieces and then spat out again. No part of it is left untouched by the havoc that has been wreaked in my life and the lives of those close to me. It is now I begin to appreciate the damage that has been done. The episode is over, but the longer term effects are just beginning.

Discovering what I have done is like waking up from a nightmare and promptly facing another one. What makes it worse, is I am responsible for this havoc, which leaves me feeling guilty and full of regrets. It is one thing to suffer my own losses, but quite another to drag those close to me into the drama too.

Whenever I am deeply manic or psychotic, I have no control over what I say or do. I am gone. Then a time comes when I am well enough to face the consequences of my words and actions. Discovering I have been unkind to my wife, made life harder for my stepson, ruined friendships, put my parents through the mill, or spent money I didn't have, is far from comfortable. Despite being well out of the worst of an episode, feelings of shame and guilt overpower me in waves, before retreating to the back of my mind to fester like boils which can't be lanced. I used to dread their unfriendly visits and didn't know what to do with these grisly emotions, so I stuffed them away in some hidden part of myself. I can't tell how much of this emotional turmoil is due to the illness and how much is my natural, human reaction to what has happened, but I do know that pushing feelings away is wearisome work and ultimately fails. The guilt I suppress one day pops up the next, as an angry outburst or a hurtful comment. Guilt also makes taking responsibility for what I have done harder to do and apologising more difficult than ever. This perpetuates the damage which began during the episode itself.

One of my biggest causes for regret came in 2005, when I was living in Australia with a group of fellow meditation teachers. These teachers were wonderful people; friendly, generous, open hearted and fun. We had a good time living together; enjoying the sunny, laidback lifestyle the East coast of Australia offers in abundance. I had been secretly lowering my lithium dose for about a year and I thought it was going well. Yet, a few days after I stopped taking my pills altogether, I fell into a state of insanity. With the protective influence of lithium no longer flowing through my veins, I became spectacularly mad. Flooded by feelings of grandiosity, elation and invincibility, this "high" felt wonderful, but it coincided with my housemates being away. So, no one was around to encourage me to get back on my pills.

I began to believe I was the Messiah and had special powers. I wandered around the house stark naked, speaking to the house plants, then licking my fingers and baptising them with my holy spit. By imparting my sacred spittle onto their delicate leaves, I believed I was bestowing a great boon upon them. I hardly slept and as the psychosis deepened, I began to experience that I was living in the bodies of all four of my housemates. Every hour on the hour, I would teleport into one of their bodies. An hour later, my wristwatch would bleep and I would become yet another of my housemates. Living five separate lives meant I showered five times a day, brushed my teeth ten times and performed all of their chores. It should have worn me out, but the mania gave me a limitless supply of energy which kept me going.

When this delusion passed, I noticed I had grown wings and could fly. Not a delusion that usually ends well. Wearing a pair of white combat pants and nothing else, I climbed onto the roof of the house and started doing handstands and cartwheels to keep myself entertained. Then it was time to try out my wings. I walked to the edge of the roof and curled my toes over the warm bitumen felt, as I prepared to throw myself into the air and soar like an eagle. Looking down onto the tarmac twenty-five feet below, I took a deep breath. This was going to be fun. I took another breath, bent my knees and…

To this day, I have no idea what stopped me from jumping and becoming a modern-day Icarus.

As I climbed down from the roof, I cut my stomach on a rusty nail and blood began to ooze from the gash. It didn't worry me; I was the Messiah and I knew exactly what to do. I strolled into the kitchen, cut a lemon in half and sterilised the dirty wound by squeezing the juice into it. It stung! I then placed some children's sticky plasters over the wound and thought nothing more of it.

At the back of our house was a lush and exotic garden, bordered by wild rainforest. From time to time, snakes and tropical birds would visit us and I would marvel at these extraordinary displays of wildlife. Right at the end of the garden was a cluster of holes in the ground, each about a centimetre in diameter, which funnel-webbed spiders had dug into the soft earth. I made a habit of steering clear of these deadly burrows, but not that day. Feeling the ecstasy of mania coarse through my body, I cartwheeled over to the holes and began to dance bare foot over them, challenging Australia's most dangerous spider to come and bite me. As the Messiah, I was immune to their venom and not for one second did I think I was risking my very survival. Funnel webs are aggressive and if untreated, their bite can kill a man in about fifteen minutes. Had even one of these nocturnal creatures braved the sunlight to defend its turf against the human feet thumping above it, I would not be around today. Had I been bitten I would not have called an ambulance or even have thought it necessary.

As I wandered back inside, the house looked more like a celestial realm than my home. Golden light shone through the windows and even a humble jar of mayonnaise, sitting on the kitchen counter, was beautiful beyond belief. Then an even stranger thing occurred. With each step I took, I shrunk a little and began to transform into a baby angel. Toddling into my housemates' bedrooms I began to roll around on their beds naked, believing I was cavorting in heavenly pastures. Rather than seeing their beds, I saw piles of lush, four-leafed clovers. Rather than feeling their cotton sheets, I felt the softest velvet imaginable. Then it all got rather disgusting. Wanting to show my appreciation to my housemates, I decided to bless their beds by urinating all over them and myself. Of course, my urine was not your everyday urine, it was an angelic fountain that consecrated whatever it touched. Once again, modesty was not a significant part of my psychotic delusions.

Later that day, one of my housemates called and the conversation we had was unusual to say the least.

"I feel fantastic," I declared. "I've been walking barefoot in the garden, making friends with the funnel-webs and doing handstands on the roof."

"Erm, I think it's a good idea to wear shoes in the garden," my housemate cautiously replied, "and please stay off the roof."

"Okay, bye," I responded jovially and hung up.

He immediately called my other housemates and told them to get home as quickly as they could. Still naked, I walked into the garden and rolled around on the lawn in full view of the neighbours who were having a barbecue. That was when the police were called, but before they arrived, my housemates came home to a house which looked like a bomb had hit it. They found me sitting on the sofa, wrapped up in kitchen paper like an Egyptian mummy, my stomach covered in bloody children's plasters, looking totally mad.

For three weeks, I was locked up in an Australian mental hospital, thousands of miles away from my family. They treated me well, but when I returned home I was depressed. Even discovering that the police were not going to prosecute me for indecent exposure couldn't cheer me up. The antipsychotics I had been given, had a similar effect to the Haloperidol I had taken years before. I became a shell of the person I was; despondent, sobbing, anxious and hopeless. My body was so stiff I could hardly move so I shuffled around like an old man, fearing I would never recover.

Whilst I had been away, my housemates had cleaned the house from top to bottom, thrown out the urine-soaked mattresses and visited me in hospital too. Their patience seemed unbreakable, with one of them even helping me into bed each night when I couldn't move my arms or hips. Their home had been violated, their personal belongings vandalised and still they helped me. If they were upset they never told me, but they had every reason to be, particularly because I had failed to tell them I was coming off my medication. I spent years carrying this guilt and for a long time I didn't muster up the courage to talk to them about what had happened. Whilst it was understandable I felt guilty, my guilt stopped me from putting things right and moving on.

Once a manic, depressive or psychotic episode seemed to be over, I harboured a fear that I might slip back into it at any moment. My family were also nervous and on high alert for any signs of me becoming ill again. This created a vicious circle, where my nervousness made them nervous and *vice versa*. Because I didn't trust myself, they became my emotional barometer and safety net. So I became preoccupied with trying to appear balanced and reasonable, tempering my positive emotions for fear of looking manic. I would have a day when I felt good again, but try to control my words and emotions, so no one thought I was moving into mania. My oversensitivity to any concern they showed put our relationship under pressure. I would get angry over their smallest comment about my state of mind. Yet I looked to them for confirmation that I was okay, whilst at the same time trying to convince them I was. This tense situation was further inflamed by me projecting my own fears onto my family, often imagining they were worried about me when they weren't.

Throughout all of my significant episodes, I was the one who got the attention and resources. I was the patient and relied heavily on my loved ones to get me through, but they didn't get the same level of support I did. They may not have been ill with bipolar, but it affected them deeply. It took their time, energy and patience. It made their lives unpredictable, at times scary and it cost money because I couldn't earn a wage whilst I was ill. They weren't trained to look after me and there were no guarantees I would ever get well, yet they supported me unconditionally. I am truly grateful for that.

There was never a specific point where I could declare, "Now, I am well." When a broken arm heals it is obvious, but with a bipolar episode the transition to wellness is less clear. My recoveries were never linear; I would have good weeks and bad weeks, stable days and tearful days. Seeming to be well for a while, I might then slip back into having symptoms. No one, including myself, knew for sure what I could or couldn't cope with and I never knew how I would be from one day to the next. My wife didn't necessarily know if she was talking to the sick or to the well Oliver, an unenviable situation to be in.

One of the biggest challenges in this part of the aftermath is being "well," but feeling shitty at the same time. I'm well enough to function normally; to shop and eat and perform everyday tasks, but I'm not myself. I want to be funny; I want to engage, I want to hang out with my friends like I do when I'm well, but I can't. Instead, I sit quietly, feeling awkward, as my mind wanders all over the place. When I'm with friends, I know I should be enjoying their company, but all I want to do is run away. When I'm alone, I know I should be enjoying my alone time, but all I want is company. The grass is always greener in this agitated state and my discomfort keeps me searching for something to make me feel better, but nothing does. I'm no longer mentally ill, but I'm unable to experience pleasure which is most frustrating. Fortunately, this state passes after a few weeks, when I am once again able to enjoy life.

During an episode, I was emotionally dependent on my wife and once I recovered, this dependency remained for some time. I looked to her for security, for confirmation, to be my confidant, my support *and* my wife. It was a lot to ask from one person and it wasn't easy for her. Over time, with persistence and patience on both our parts, I sorted myself out and my confidence returned. This process of inching my way back to good health and rebuilding myself invariably took longer than I expected. The aftereffects of medication and the chemical disruption in my brain weighed on me heavily. My nervous system had been put under excessive strain and my brain didn't work well at all. I was foggy, forgetful and easily overwhelmed, but I was determined to recover and this determination drove me on.

It would be natural to assume that whilst the episodes were destructive, the periods in between were okay; and in some ways this was true. I experienced stability for good lengths of time; I got a university degree, travelled all over the world and held down a job, but even though I was not obviously ill, I was still affected by bipolar. For example, when I worked as a sales trader, I saved up about £40,000 and then inherited an even larger sum of money. At the same time, I became hypomanic and metamorphosed from conscientious saver to profligate spender. I started to believe money was going to magically appear whenever I needed it. At the same time, a rather odd taxi driver told me the world was going to end and – since I believed him – I was given another reason not to invest. Rather than investing a healthy chunk, as would have been my inclination when well, I decided to keep all of my money in my current account, whilst I lived off it for six years. I spent some money on myself and too much of it I gave away. Even when well, my decision-making abilities and the way I viewed the world was far from normal. My bipolar bifocals blended mania's false optimism with depression's pessimism, giving me two ridiculous reasons to spend all of my money.

Six years later, I was broke. I didn't have any savings, stocks, shares, premium bonds or property and I hadn't put an ounce of energy into building a career. Had I invested wisely, my wife and I would now have a healthy income for the rest of our lives.

It wasn't solely my financial life which went astray between episodes. I also became a compulsive risk taker. On one occasion, after I was thrown out of a nightclub for getting into a dust up, I found myself climbing up the side of the Royal Freeman General Hospital in Newcastle, like an inebriated spiderman heading for the roof.

"Oi, you, get down," a security guard shouted from below.

Feeling unusually obedient, I climbed down.

"Stay here," he told me, "I've called the police."

The portly security guard was not in great shape and as soon as he dropped his guard, I sprinted off into the night. As I remember it; I ran for some time, then dived over a hedge and hid, feeling rather pleased with myself. As the security guard must remember it; Spider Idiot stumbled a few yards, before tripping over his own feet and falling headfirst into a flower bed. The security guard then wandered over to where I was sprawled and sat on my back, waiting for the police to arrive.

"I'm sorry," I told the custody sergeant at the station, "I'm a manic depressive. Sometimes I get carried away when I have a couple of drinks."

The policeman let me go with a warning, but similar incidents continued as time went on. I jumped off bridges at night into water of unknown depth and I walked under an articulated lorry as it was driving down a busy London road. If I could find a way to get a kick, I would kick.

There were other limitations which came between episodes that I had not anticipated. In my final year of university, my Commanding Officer in the OTC encouraged me to apply for the Royal Marines. I had wanted to be a Marine since I was twelve and I couldn't believe I had been put forward for it. Two interviews later, I was set to attend their Officer Selection Course, but as I filled out the application form, a question appeared on the page in front of me and my heart sank.

"Have you ever had, or do you suffer from any form of mental illness?"

I so wanted to write "no," but I couldn't. This was too important.

Then, with a heavy heart and an air of foreboding, I read the next question.

"Do you take any form of medication?"

The application form lay on my desk for a week, as I pondered ways of getting around those questions, but I came up short.

Two weeks after I had sent in my application, I received a reply, informing me that taking psychiatric medication precluded me from applying to the Marines. Had I failed the course, I would have been disappointed, but to not get the opportunity to prove myself was a slug in the guts. From where I stand now, I understand why the Marines rejected me and I think it was the correct decision.

I dusted myself down and decided to go for plan B, which was to study medicine and become a doctor. Sure enough, on one of the last pages of the application form, the dreaded question appeared.

"Have you ever had, or do you suffer from any form of mental illness?"

I had the grades, the work experience and the references, but I was rejected by all of the medical schools I applied to without being given a single interview.

For the next twenty-five years, rejection was to be a constant companion in my attempts to build a successful career. After the medical schools shunned me, I knew bipolar would stop me from pursuing certain avenues, but I wasn't prepared for how my physical state would hold me back too. I gave many jobs my best shot, but I invariably failed because my physical capacity was so reduced. I have not managed to work full time since my mid-twenties and a successful career has thus far evaded me. Over time, these repeated failures took their toll and I gave up hope of having a proper career. I blamed myself for this because, after all, I was the common denominator.

Bipolar's impact on my relationships was lousy too. In the middle of a psychosis, I once joyfully told my wife I desired to have sex with other women; one of whom she knew. At the time, I was living in a world inhabited by erotic, leather clad angels and I had no idea who my wife was, but that didn't stop my words from hurting her. It isn't easy to be hurt by someone who loves you and then rationalise their behaviour as mental illness, but over time she did. It is unfair to expect someone to understand that the actions of a mentally ill person are not *their* actions, but the actions of an illness, but over time she understood that too. When I was out of psychosis, she wanted to talk to me about what I had said, but I became defensive and we ended up having a fight. I would eventually lower my defenses, but it took time.

It was many weeks before I accepted that my thirteen-year-old stepson had been scared by my psychosis and had suffered because he couldn't be at home when I was very ill. I was no longer a source of stability for him and much of his mother's attention had been directed towards me. He had understandably felt neglected. Yet, because I felt so guilty, I couldn't see his viewpoint and clung to the belief I was the only one who had suffered. This added to the awkward atmosphere at home.

Fortunately, as a family we created the opportunity to heal the damage. When I felt mentally and emotionally well enough, we all sat down together and talked through the whole episode, how we felt and how it had affected us. When we talked, we were conscious of not interrupting each other, which created an open and receptive atmosphere. My wife and stepson expressed how challenging it had been for them and I was able to take in their words without defending myself. I apologised for what I had put them through and told them how grateful I was to have them.

I needed to be humble enough to see their side of the story because, had I argued with them, my apology would have meant nothing. During that conversation, whether it was bipolar's fault or mine was irrelevant, I needed to take responsibility and not blame the illness for what had occurred. When I did this, the most incredible thing happened. As soon as I had apologised, my wife said,

"It wasn't your fault. You were ill."

My stepson nodded in agreement.

I was overwhelmed by how forgiving they were. I had blamed myself, but their willingness to listen and forgive me, made all the difference. At the same time, I realised they had been carrying me for a long time and I needed to step up and be a good husband and stepfather again. Throughout the episode I had only thought about myself, but now I needed to think about them.

Talking can be helpful if our words are chosen wisely. Listening is invaluable if we truly listen. My apology, together with their loving and forgiving attitudes, laid the foundation for a healing of our relationships and a strengthening of them too.

I have now been well for over five years, but at times bipolar still affects my relationships negatively. I go through periods of being very moody and sometimes say unkind things that I don't mean. This can drive people away. My views can also be more extreme than they normally are and I sometimes express them abrasively. When this happens, it feels like it is the only way to release an intensity that is filling my body. This intensity makes it hard for me to settle into being my normal friendly self, which is frustrating as I want to be a nice guy. When I emerge from my funk and realise what I have done, the best thing I can do is apologise.

Learnings:

1. Bipolar's damage isn't limited to the manic, depressive and psychotic episodes themselves. It can affect every part of my life, even when I am well.

2. Feeling guilty made it harder for me to take responsibility for what I had done and more difficult to apologise.

3. Those who were close to me also suffered greatly from my episodes.

4. One of the biggest challenges is being "well" enough to function, but feeling constantly shitty and unable to enjoy everyday life.

5. Apologising to my family for the hurt I had caused was very important. It healed wounds which otherwise may never have healed.

6. There came a time when I had to let go of being the patient and return to my role as a stepfather and husband. This could only occur once I had recovered from the worst of the episode. It took courage, but was worth it, and allowed my family life to return to normal.

Chapter 9. A dance with death

"Don't know how I kept going. You just do. You have to, so you do."

– Elizabeth Wein.

I was fifteen when my mother told me my grandmother had killed herself; and before that day I don't recall ever thinking about the subject of suicide. In my fifteenth year, over 7,000 people took their own life in the UK [18], but I wasn't directly affected by any of these deaths. So when I heard my grandmother had lost a long battle with manic depression, I didn't know what to think. Before that day, I might have judged a person who killed themselves as weak; someone who couldn't hack the challenges of life, but when faced with a situation so close to home I didn't feel that way. I felt sad my grandmother had been so unhappy and I felt sorry for my mother who had lost her mother in her early twenties. Life went on and I rarely thought about my grandmother's suicide or why she did it. Little did I know, within a couple of years I would be fighting my own battle with suicide, whilst facing the same merciless illness which had taken my grandmother's life.

When I was under suicide watch in the Royal Edinburgh Hospital, the muscles in my body were so contorted by Haloperidol they wouldn't respond to my commands. I couldn't eat or go to the toilet without the help of a nurse and I felt indescribably desperate. It was in the midst of this experience, that I told my parents something no parent would ever want to hear.

"I want to kill myself," I spluttered through tearful sobs, my words spitting darkness into an already dark well. But although I believed I did, I didn't want to die. What I wanted was for my suffering to end and death seemed the only viable option. At the time, living was so unspeakably unbearable that dying appeared to be my only hope of release. My words gave me the sense I had some sort of control over my world, a way to fight what was happening inside me, but they cut into the hearts of the two people I loved the most. I hoped that by telling my parents how wretched I felt, I could somehow drag them into my world and feel less alone. It was a cry for help rather than a threat because I had no way of taking my own life at the time. Had my mother and father known this it would have been easier for them. Instead, the pressure of seeing me so ill was compounded by the real possibility I might not survive the illness. [19]

In those dark days, I would have done anything to make myself feel better, but nothing did. Nothing anyone could say was able to take away the pain. No one could dispel my loneliness because it was the loneliness of depression, not the loneliness which comes from a lack of companionship.

In each of my depressive episodes there were times when I wanted to kill myself, but no matter how bad the episodes were, I never tried. Why was this? I'm not entirely sure, but below are some of the factors which probably saved me:

1. The depression itself: The very beast that made me suicidal also kept me alive because during my worst depressions I was too ill to commit suicide. I didn't have the energy to crawl out of bed, let alone accomplish the Herculean task of getting hold of enough sleeping pills. Living in a mental hospital helped me too. Ward one was a safe place with caring staff who kept a close eye on me. It would have been nearly impossible for me to take my own life without them seeing the warning signs. If they suspected a patient might hurt themselves, the patient was immediately put on suicide watch and had a nurse with them at all times.

As I recovered from the depression, my desire to die lessened and my vitality returned. Although I was not nearly as down as I had been, I was still in a precarious situation, because I now had the energy and means to kill myself if I really wanted to. No longer within the safe confines of a mental hospital, no one could stop me from taking my own life if I decided to. Although suicidal thoughts still entered my mind, as the last semblance of depression snarled at me menacingly, they didn't affect me in the way they had done before. They no longer had that power. This was fortunate because I was now strong enough to ignore them and death was no longer a tempting solution.

I think the most helpful thing I learned from this experience was that depression comes to an end. None of my depressions, not even the most stubborn, lasted forever. Knowing this has given me more patience and fortitude whilst caught in the midst of one.

2. Love: Love played a powerful role in keeping me alive, but I have yet to see the mainstream medical community give its benefits the attention it deserves. When exposed to love, we humans benefit in a myriad of ways, but as far as psychiatry is concerned this factor is largely overlooked. If the benefits of love were consciously harnessed in psychiatric treatment, I believe it would speed up the recovery process of many a patient and prevent others from becoming ill. This would require money, staff and training because expressing love requires time and awareness. If doctors and nurses are overstretched, they don't have enough time with their patients to express love in a meaningful way. With enough time on their hands, the staff would have the opportunity to be as kind, loving and attentive as they wanted to be.

I believe doctors, nurses and managers need to be educated in the role of love in psychiatric treatment. Not because they are not loving enough already, but because learning more about love's impact would empower them. Officially supporting a policy of love would be rewarding for everyone and would save lives and money. It is fascinating to see how much more loving people become, when they know their lovingness makes a difference.

Imagine working in a hospital where love is the top priority, where all employees are encouraged to value love. A place where love is acknowledged as an instrumental part of treatment. Many of the staff who have looked after me over the years expressed a great deal of love, but I felt they expressed it because they themselves were loving people, not because the system was set up to support it. If the system valued love, the love expressed would expand and everyone would benefit.

I think the physical environment plays an important part in the healing process. Many times, I have walked into a mental hospital or psychiatrist's office and it was like walking into a dentist's treatment room. There are many things which can be done to uplift the decour; decorating wards with bright pictures and fresh flowers, allowing pets into psychiatric units and having flexible visiting hours are just the tip of the iceberg. Anything that transforms an environment from sterile and cold, to homely and welcoming, lifts people's spirits and encourages healing.

After a talk I gave for a group of psychiatrists in Norway, one of them came up to me, clearly touched by what I had said. With tears in his eyes, he told me he worked with some of the sickest people in the country and hadn't realised how much of a difference his love could make to them. Because his patients were sent to other units as soon as they were no longer critically ill, he never knew the impact he had or if they had ever recovered. Because of this he was feeling despondent and contemplating giving psychiatry up. My talk inspired him to consciously explore love when he was treating his patients and it gave him a renewed sense of purpose. He told me he couldn't wait to get back to his ward to experiment with this novel idea. All it took to inspire him was to be made aware of the importance and value of the love he already possessed.

If anyone is loving or creates a loving environment around them, a field of love is generated and this field is contagious. This may sound a little strange to some, but really it is obvious. If you go to a party where one person is silently holding a grudge, it pulls the whole party down. If you go to a party where someone is in love, it uplifts the room. Loving people interact with life in a positive way.

They spread good vibes and optimism effortlessly. People like them and trust them; and by giving love away they magnify it. Love is a win-win. The more you give away the more you receive.

The field of love is healing in itself. It uplifts people, makes them feel safe and comforts them, all of which aid the healing process. If a patient is surrounded by love, I believe they are more likely to emerge from their depression or psychological challenge in one piece. A loving field can be catalysed by a simple loving act. Even if we don't feel particularly loving, by acting in loving ways we still cultivate the field and strengthen it. Even small acts of love can have a great impact. The nurses who spoke kindly to me when they opened my curtains in the morning, or the doctor who took the time to give me a guided relaxation, did so out of the goodness of their hearts and helped me along the way.

Love is obviously important outside the hospital walls too. It is easy to get caught up in the chaos of life, but if we notice someone is struggling, then we have an opportunity to expand love. Calling a friend, smiling at a stranger, or taking time to listen to someone who needs to talk, can change and save lives. Someone who is vulnerable and needs to connect may not have the confidence or mental strength to initiate anything for themselves. Ask them out for a cup of coffee; it can make all the difference to them and will probably make you feel good too.

Outside close relationships, it is common to be wary of showing love. We may not be comfortable expressing love until someone expresses it first, but this is the wrong way round. If we wait, perhaps other people will wait too and then no one will be brave enough to make the first move. Love first, ask questions later.

The hospital visits I received were acts of love, which connected me to the outside world and to the life to which I wanted to return. Those visits showed me I wasn't forgotten and would get home at some point. They kept me going and speeded my recovery.

3. Giving: When I got out of hospital, one of the first responsibilities I had was to take care of my family's two dogs. This task was exactly what I needed. I was still nervous and irritable around people, but not those dogs. They didn't judge me or worry about me becoming ill again. No matter how poorly I felt, they wagged their tails and nuzzled me affectionately. I fed them and took them on long runs in the countryside. The combination of the exercise, their company and being in nature gave me such a boost.

Every night my wire-haired dachshund Monty slept in my bed, like a long, furry hot water bottle. If I awoke in the night, I wasn't alone. Those two hairy creatures needed me and I needed them. This responsibility was transformative, as it put me in a state of giving rather than taking. Giving has the power to draw a person out of their negative mindset and to make them happier. You can try it for yourself. If you feel a bit flat, or worried, or bored, pick up the phone and ring someone who might need a call. Or get up and tidy the house as a surprise for your partner or parents. Nine times out of ten you will feel the better for it.

4. Resilience: Many people with mental illness possess an inner resilience. This resilience won't allow me to kill myself. It is a stubborn, unyielding, safety mechanism, fuelled by a gritty determination which has kept me going when faced with my greatest challenges.

As an impetuous twenty-one-year-old, I was talked into running the London Marathon by some friends. I agreed, but it was only five weeks before the race, which didn't give me nearly enough time to train properly.

The day of the race was swelteringly hot and I shot off at break-neck speed, eating up the first thirteen miles with ease. At mile fourteen, I unceremoniously hit the wall and it all went wrong. My legs cramped, my feet blistered and I bruised my toenails so badly that five of them fell off the following week. My dastardly mind spared me no quarter.

"Quit you idiot!"

"Give up, loser."

"You're never going to make it."

I did my best to ignore its gloomy ramblings and dragged myself around the remaining twelve miles, sobbing with tears of frustration as I did. I eventually finished the race and even though everything had seemed to be against me, I didn't quit. This same resilience helped get me through my depressions.

Resilience isn't necessarily a trait people are born with, but it can be developed. Sometimes we develop it consciously and sometimes life develops it for us, by throwing challenges at us unasked. For me, physical and mental challenges have all built up resilience. As did my father encouraging me to be brave and adventurous.

Perhaps the most obvious resilience builder was bipolar itself. No other hardships have come close to what that has put me through. Large parts of society believe easy is best, which can be true. Yet a life without challenge so easily becomes boring and unfulfilling. To find ways to push ourselves out of our comfort zone can build resilience which is invaluable.

5. Medication: When I was suicidal for long periods of time, I couldn't have survived without antidepressants to drag me into a functioning state of mind. Of course, antidepressants have side-effects and there is no guarantee they will work, but they have worked well for me in the past. Taking lithium has also prevented me from becoming depressed and suicidal, which means it has played a major role in keeping me alive.

6. Fear: When push came to shove, fear played a part in stopping me from killing myself. What would happen after I died? What if death didn't end my anguish? What if I went to hell? Not knowing the answers to these questions scared me and discouraged me from doing anything rash.

When I was in a moderate depression, the fear of hurting my family dissuaded me from committing suicide. I hated the thought of putting them through that. Yet when I was severely depressed, I no longer cared about how my family felt because the condition wouldn't let me care. It had overwhelmed every part of my brain, including the parts which cared about my loved ones. This may sound callous, but it isn't meant that way. In deep depressions, no place exists for me to consider my "friends'" or "families'" feelings. No matter how much I love them, hurting them isn't enough to stop me from wanting to kill myself. This isn't my conscious choice; it is the depression poisoning my mind.

Relatives and friends suffer a great deal after a loved one has killed themself. They will never see their loved one again and won't have their support or companionship for the rest of their life. They often feel they could have done more to help; and their suffering may be compounded by their inability to understand why their loved one did it. They are left with questions as to why their son, daughter, father, mother, husband, or wife committed suicide and they often find no answers.

Some are left blaming themselves or looking for someone else to blame. Many are left in very challenging situations; with debt, raising children on their own and a burden of guilt, but a few of the problems they may face. This can naturally lead to anger and resentment towards the person who has taken their own life, which may last for years. How could they have been so selfish? How could they have deserted me and left me with such a mess to clear up? The tendency is to look for a rational answer as to why they did it, but one isn't necessarily there to be found.

When I was suicidal, depression robbed me of rational thought. My brain didn't work. If I had committed suicide, would I have killed myself? Or would depression have killed me?

Due to my own dance with suicidal tendencies, I would like to change the expression, "so and so killed themselves," to, "so and so died from depression." It's a small thing, but it implies the person who died did not do it of their own rational choice. The depression took over and forced them to do it. I think if the relatives and friends who were left behind knew that sometimes there was no rational choice in the matter, it might help them to come to terms with it.

Learnings:

1. The times when I most wanted to die were also the times when I wasn't capable of committing suicide (due to being in hospital, and my physical and mental state).

2. When I said, "I want to die," what I really meant was "I want my suffering to end."

3. Knowing that depression doesn't last forever helps me to get through them.

4. Love is not something that can be scientifically quantified and is rarely even considered, but a powerful healing tool.

5. Being given responsibility and being encouraged to give to others was very good for me.

6. Resilience can be developed voluntarily and from the challenges of life. It is a significant advantage to develop resilience.

7. Medication has been necessary for me since my first episode.

8. From my perspective, the expression "so and so killed themselves," is not as accurate as, "so and so died from depression."

Chapter 10. Side effects

"The road to hell is paved with good intentions."

– Saint Bernard of Clairvaux, Cistercian Abbot.

For the first ten years I took lithium (1994-2004), I didn't have any resistance to taking the drug. In fact, I was grateful for it. Lithium did a remarkably good job of keeping me out of mania, psychosis and depression. As far as I was concerned, I had found the solution to bipolar and was prepared to keep going with it indefinitely. For those ten years, I rarely missed a dose. I trusted Dr. Wrate and I trusted lithium, so there was no inner conflict for me.

After university I was able to embark on a high-flying career in an investment bank. As an equities sales trader, the hours were long, the office frenzied and lunch was for wimps. I am told it is common for people with bipolar to be attracted to stressful jobs which are not suited to their wellbeing, but tempting to their manic minds. This was certainly the case for me. It was an odd career choice for someone who was arithmetically challenged, creative and liked to be outdoors.

All day long, I sat in front of six computer screens, two phones on either side of my desk and televisions hanging above my head blaring out all the bad news Fox and CNN could muster. Clients were demanding, millions of dollars passed through my trading desk each day and a big mistake could end up costing me my career.

Although it wasn't a job I was naturally suited to, I saw it as a golden opportunity to invest in my long term plan of being happy. My plan was to work my tail off for about ten years, buy a place on the beach in Thailand and live there. Who wouldn't be at peace in a tropical paradise with lots of money in the bank? Although I didn't enjoy the job itself, working towards this dream gave me a reason to get out of bed at five o'clock in the morning and a sense of purpose which made it bearable. Yet, unknown to me, I was struggling with the side effects of lithium. My memory for stocks and numbers was poor and I found it hard to control my temper. I even picked a fight with another trader because he was a bully and I was having a bad day. The stress that fired up my colleagues ate away at me, I lost weight and became chronically tired. After three years I resigned; stressed out, bored and exhausted.

At that time, I had been stable for five years and bipolar was a distant memory I rarely thought about. I lived in a peaceful part of London; the pressure was off and I planned to take some time to discover what I was *really* meant to be doing with my life. I studied yoga and massage and ate in some of London's finest restaurants, but with or without the condition, I felt listless and lost.

My outer world was very comfortable, but my inner world continued to challenge me. Not only did I have a bipolar brain that bounced around of its own accord, but I was used to the buzz of the trading floor and a sedate life was too uneventful for my overactive mind. I had swapped the stress of the trading floor for a bland and unfulfilling life of leisure. Young, ambitious men don't do well when their life lacks purpose.

Since I was small, I had a sense there was something significant I was meant to do with my life, but what it was remained a mystery to me. One day whilst walking past the windmill on Wimbledon Common, it finally dawned on me; I wanted peace. Even as a sales trader in the hardened aorta of the heart of Capitalism, peace had been my ultimate goal. My goal was pure, but my method had been flawed. I thought I could buy happiness, but I couldn't. It is commonly known that money can't make you happy, but although most people pretend to agree, deep down, they don't really believe it. The majority of people are still chasing money so they can be happy at some point in the future. That day on the Common, it became apparent that a place on the beach wasn't going to bring me peace because I would still have the same head on my shoulders, a head which was far from peaceful. No, I had to find another way.

One thing led to another and on a summery weekend in Glastonbury I learned a powerful form of meditation that was to change me forever. In the months which followed, I began to rediscover a peaceful awareness I had known as a child. I became happier, my troubled mind calmer and life seemed rosier for no reason. The meditation gave me a sense of purpose because it was obviously making me into a better version of myself and this was encouraging.

A year later, at the end of 2003, I decided to go on a six-month retreat in the mountains of British Columbia. The retreat was run by monks who had dedicated their lives to serving humanity by finding and spreading peace. It was a happy, vibrant place, attracting all sorts of people from all over the world. I enjoyed the sense of community and the idea that we were all focused on one thing and it didn't take long before I became a monk too.

Some of the participants on the retreat were alternative healers and when I told them I had bipolar and was taking lithium, they weren't impressed. They saw psychiatry as a crude and old-fashioned approach, which did patients more harm than good.

"Psychiatrists don't cure mental illness, they just put a lid on your emotions with drugs," one told me sternly.

"Lithium is toxic," said another.

As an alternative to the evils of conventional medicine, they variously recommended; shamanism, homeopathy, herbal remedies, supplements, acupuncture, distance healing, reiki… to name but a few. I was overcome with enthusiasm for my new world, but my enthusiasm clouded my judgement. I had no idea these healers were expressing their own prejudices, rather than speaking the truth and I took their words at face value. My resolve to stay on lithium for the rest of my days began to weaken.

To add momentum to my newly acquired doubt, I read a book whose author claimed meditation could heal all physical and mental illness. He was a well-regarded spiritual teacher and seemed to be offering me a way of living without lithium. I was also influenced by other teachers who were critical of conventional medicine. Everywhere I turned, I faced situations that seemed to be tempting me to come off lithium.

After many years of psychiatric and alternative treatments, I am aware of some of the failings of psychiatric medicine, but the alternative movement is no panacea for mental illness either. Different people respond to different treatments and to make bold claims to anyone about how their condition should be treated is foolish. Those healers may have known alternative methods to treat bipolar, but they didn't know anything about me and they shouldn't have been casting doubt on my medication in casual conversations. Psychiatry is by no means perfect, but it does stop tens of thousands of people killing themselves each year and has helped me enormously. The road to hell is paved with good intentions and thanks to those healers' good intentions, I began to think perhaps I had already cured bipolar with meditation and I no longer needed lithium. I was to pay a high price for listening to them.

Untreated, bipolar is an unforgiving condition and has a habit of coming back in progressively aggressive forms. [20] This is one of the reasons why many people choose to put up with the unpleasant side effects of medication. Some people can't accept that they need to take psychiatric medication, particularly for a long time and anyone who has been on it will understand why. The side effects can be tough, sometimes worse than the illness itself and there can be a confusing conflict between needing medication and perhaps no longer needing it. Some patients will take their pills for a while, but once they feel better, they stop, which is understandable. Searching for alternatives to unpleasant psychiatric medication is, in my opinion, a valid course of action. If I could find a treatment; conventional or alternative, which worked as well as lithium but had fewer or no side effects, I would jump on it. However, this should be done with the help of qualified medical professionals and not on a whim. Tampering with medication should not be done lightly, as the outcome can be catastrophic.

On that meditation retreat in the mountains of British Columbia, thousands of miles away from my family and friends; I started to lower my lithium dose, without consulting a doctor or a psychiatrist or having any type of medical support. I was both excited and nervous about tampering with lithium, but I thought I would give it a go. No one thought reducing my medication in a foreign country, without psychiatric support, was idiotic and if they did they didn't say. I certainly wasn't wise enough to realise this for myself. The sensible idea of waiting until I got home and seeking medical supervision didn't even cross my mind.

As I lowered my dose, a sense of anxiety began to build. A few days later, whilst practicing yoga in the retreat centre, I witnessed two colleagues transform into dragons right in front of my eyes. The dragons were squat, muscular and covered in silvery-green scales, that shone brightly as they paced around impatiently. One of them yawned, revealing rows of dagger-like teeth and a forked tongue that darted in and out. Before I could do anything, both sets of reptilian eyes caught sight of me and the dragons ran in my direction, intent on having me for lunch. Scared half to death, I sprinted to my dormitory and slammed the door behind me. My heart pounding, I fumbled to find a box of lithium and a glass of water and gulped two and a half pills down my neck. Within a few hours, my fear had subsided and the hallucinations had stopped.

Two months later I tried again, this time lowering my dose more cautiously. Back in the same yoga room, another of the students transformed into a purple snake, with florescent venom dripping from its fangs and a wicked twinkle in its jet-black eyes. After another panicked dash to the safety of my dorm, with more than a touch of *déjà vu*, I scrambled for my box of lithium and went back to my original dose.

After these two experiences, you would think I would give up on my dream of a life without lithium, but I didn't. I had got the idea into my head and it had stuck.

Two years later in Australia, I tried to come of lithium once more (see Chapter 8), but this ended so disastrously that I saw sense and gave up my futile quest…

For a while.

Eight years later

In the spring of 2011, I was invited to be a case study for a group of trainee homeopaths in Oslo. When I told the group I was taking lithium, a gasp swept through the room.

"You know lithium's a toxic medicine?" one of the students asked pointedly.

Memories of my failed attempts to come off lithium flooded back. I felt I had been hijacked, but rather than walk out of the room, curiosity got the better of me. A long discussion ensued and I listened to it intently. The students' arguments against the use of lithium were compelling and they suggested homeopathic remedies to replace my medication. They sounded exactly like the alternative healers in Canada and once again I was exposed to a world where lithium was the enemy. What made the situation different this time, was that over the years, I had gradually experienced more and more side effects and my life was more limited than it had ever been. Thanks to the side effects and to those well-meaning homeopathy students, my incentive to come off lithium was once again fired up.

The side effects I lived with at that time were:

1. Emotional disconnection (see Chapter 4).

2. Poor memory and concentration: Before lithium, my brain had been razor sharp, but now my head was filled with fog. I had to give up reading books because my brain couldn't absorb the words or follow a simple story. I would read a sentence and by the time I had got to the end of it, I had forgotten the beginning. It took me seven years to learn to speak a very basic level of Norwegian, which is something many foreigners do in a few months.

Oslo is a small city, but I sometimes got lost within a hundred metres of my flat, not knowing where I was or where I was going. It was hard for me to move forward in life because I couldn't get my head around situations and my ability to move forward in life was reduced.

3. Irritation and aggression: On lithium, I could never properly relax and was more irritable and aggressive. This was challenging for my personal relationships.

4. Hallucinations (see Chapter 7).

5. Exhaustion: Once a week, I had to spend a day or two in bed. I couldn't train, play sport or carry heavy luggage without experiencing days of exhaustion afterwards. I was less motivated than I had ever been and found it difficult to start new projects, keep a job or take initiatives.

6. Creativity: Once I was on lithium, my creativity pretty much disappeared. I had been a good artist, but was no longer able to sit down to draw or paint. My hands were too stiff and my body and mind unable to relax into what had been a peaceful and enjoyable hobby. It seemed the sensitivity I needed to create was also no longer available to me.

7. Muscle stiffness/weakness: From the age of twenty-five, my muscles ached and sometimes I could barely pick up a chair. I lost dexterity in my hands and hurt myself doing simple tasks such as opening jam jars.

8. Psoriasis, sinus problems, tinnitus, tremors, light sensitivity and blurred vision.

9. Dehydration and overheating: Lithium seemed to raise my body temperature. In winter, when my friends wore jackets and boots; I was often in a t-shirt. I was almost always thirsty and downed glasses of water like they were going out of fashion.

There seems to be a big difference in how people react to taking lithium. I asked fifty lithium users about their experiences with the drug and most said it controlled their illness effectively. A few experienced a similar level of side effects to me, but the majority had side effects which were bearable and, in a couple of cases, non-existent. One even called it her "miracle drug." It is important for me to state, from what I have seen and experienced, psychiatric medications affect different people in different ways. Some positive, some negative. I do not want the readers of this book to assume that their experience with lithium would be similar to mine.

Learnings:

1. The idea of becoming medication free was enticing and I became very stubborn in my pursuit of it.

2. When it comes to psychiatric medication, giving throwaway advice can have damaging consequences. A mentally ill person's judgment may not be up to par, or they may be blinded by the opportunity to be side effect free, leaving them vulnerable to other people's opinions.

3. My side effects got worse over time.

4. I didn't appreciate how dangerous it was to come off medication without the appropriate support.

5. The side effects of lithium vary from person to person. Some experience debilitating side effects, others don't.

Chapter 11. Coming off medication

"Lithium accumulates in the bodily tissues and tends to accumulate the most in the brain and kidneys. It builds up to a lesser extent in the thyroid, bones, muscles and liver."

– Medical News Today.

Here is a short exercise you might want to try:

Imagine you discover you have a terminal disease. You are told it is aggressive and if left untreated, you only have a few months to live.

The good news is there's a drug that can control the disease indefinitely, but this drug has considerable disadvantages. You will have to take it every day for the rest of your life and the side effects are so grim that you won't be able to exercise or work again. It will drive your illness into remission, but your body will ache, you will have headaches, your concentration will be limited and your memory depleted. You will no longer have any contact with your emotions, which means you won't feel love for your partner or your children. In short, this drug will seriously limit your life and inhibit what you can do. What would you do? Would you take it or not?

You might decide to give this medicine a miss and spend the last months of your life with the people you love. Or you might take the medication and deal with the side effects as best as you can.

Now, imagine you have been on the medication for a few years. The illness has disappeared! The drug has worked! Then out of the blue, people you trust start telling you that you might not need the medication. They tell you about other solutions which are easier on your body, which have few, if any, side effects. What would you do? Would you keep living your life at this significantly reduced level or would you take the risk and come off the drug?

"Why would you want to stop taking a medicine that's controlling your illness?" my Edinburgh doctor asked me impatiently. I told her about lithium's side effects, but she didn't seem to take them onboard. "It's best left well alone. All medicines have side effects," she snapped. "People who come off their medication can get extremely ill."

By talking to a professional, I thought I was doing the right thing, but she showed me no empathy. She seemed to have made up her mind before we had even had a proper conversation. Even if my idea was foolish, it was not one I was willing to put aside because of a stern glance or a disapproving comment. This was important to me. It was my life we were talking about. I needed to talk through my options and for my doctor to take my dilemma seriously. Above all, I needed to be heard. I left her office feeling frustrated. It had been like talking to a brick wall.

It is a challenge for anyone who has not taken psychiatric medication to understand fully the dilemma of medication *versus* no medication. If you have not personally experienced the effects and side effects of psychiatric drugs, you cannot know what they are like. You may have studied them, or even be an expert in this field, but if you haven't taken the pills day after day, month after month, then you have no direct experience of what these medications are truly like.

Knowing about something and experiencing it are different. Knowing involves gathering knowledge and can be done through reading, studying, observing, or even watching documentaries. Experience can only be gained by being immersed in a situation and living through it for yourself. It is the difference between watching hours of professional boxing on YouTube and getting into a ring and going eight rounds with a middleweight. These words are not meant to belittle psychiatrists and psychologists, whose knowledge of mental illness helps patients all over the world. They are meant to gently remind them that although they know *about* medication, most have no direct experience of taking it. A health professional's competence, experience and knowledge are clearly relevant, but listening to what the patient has to say and learning from it, may be what separates a psychiatrist from a great psychiatrist.

Over the years, I have met doctors who believed they had all the answers and didn't use me, the patient, as a resource. They didn't ask the right questions, or if they did, they didn't really listen to my answers. In fact, they hardly listened to me at all. They seemed to be interested solely in what *they* knew; taking whatever I said and fitting it into their way of seeing mental illness. They were the doctor, I was the patient, they knew best, I didn't. It doesn't matter who you are, listening is an art form worth cultivating because none of us know all the answers.

In 2021, the total number of people taking psychiatric drugs in the United States was just shy of 77 million (of which

6.2 million were under 18 years old).[21] Despite the vast number of people taking medication and the side effects that can come with it, we live in a society which has little tolerance for psychiatric patients who come off their medication. The prevailing view is that it is a foolish thing to do, yet the average person knows little about these drugs.

It is a complex situation because there are valid reasons why psychiatric patients desire a medication-free life and there are valid reasons why society doesn't want mentally ill people harming themselves or others. Whilst society's fear is understandable, I believe each case should be examined on its own merits rather than dismissed out of hand. The value of listening to a patient from a balanced and open perspective cannot be overstated.

Some of the doctors I have met acted like overprotective parents, stifling me with their good intentions. They seemed so afraid of the consequences of reducing medication that they refused to discuss the matter at length, hoping instead to scare me into forgetting about it. I was a grown man and didn't respond well to this approach. When I told them what I wanted to do, I would see them tense up and start the process of dissuading me without giving me the opportunity to elaborate. Trying to suppress my desire was like trying to hold a beach ball underwater in a swimming pool. Those doctors could force it beneath the surface for a while, but at some point, it would shoot out with great force. Controlling people, even with the best of intentions, isn't wise.

It is common to view the desire to come off medication as part of the psychiatric condition. This can certainly be true, but is not always the case. When I talked to those overprotective doctors, I was stable and well. What I needed was a doctor who would treat my desire to be lithium free as valid, not necessarily to agree with it, but to be willing to talk it through. Had I been able to have a balanced discussion with such a doctor, I might have decided to stay on lithium. Instead, I was left to figure out my dilemma by myself.

A few months later, in Oslo, I found a psychiatrist who was willing to help me lower my dose. I didn't much like her, but I knew I needed professional help if I was going to have any chance of success.

A couple of weeks after I started lowering my dose, I began to feel anxious. Over the phone, my new psychiatrist told me my blood test showed that I was a little below the therapeutic range and I should go back to my original dose. I wasn't prepared to give up so quickly, but rather than discuss this with me, she became frustrated and so did I. I never went back to see her again. With hindsight, I should have called it quits. The dismissive approaches of my psychiatrist and doctor were not what I wanted to hear, but they would prove to be correct. The unfortunate by-product of their attitude was that it pushed me further away from the medical establishment at a time when I should have been close to it. Coming off lithium by myself was no longer an option, I had tried that one, so I made an appointment with a well-known homeopath in Oslo.

"If you keep taking that much lithium, at some point you could have kidney failure. We can lower your dose gradually and I'll support you on the way down with remedies. I'm sure we'll be able to get you off it," the homeopath told me confidently. His office was in the same street as the psychiatrist's, but his tone and words could not have been further from hers.

His first remedy sent me into a three-day panic attack.

"That was a common reaction," he told me at our next appointment. "You're experiencing the emotions that ordinary people have. They're frightening because you're not used to them. Lithium has suppressed your feelings for years and now they're coming out. You'll get through this."

The theory that suppressed emotions are stored in the body and are released once a patient stops taking psychiatric medicine, is common amongst alternative healers. Back then I accepted it at face value, but now I am not so sure it is true. Lithium suppressed my emotions, or at least stopped me from feeling them, but I'm not convinced they were then stored in my body in perpetuity. If they had been, then presumably my joyful and loving emotions should have come out too? And yet – as I'm sure my wife would gladly attest – those particular emotions were distinctly absent.

After six months of fear and instability, I tried another homeopath.

"Your emotions have been held down for years and they need to come out. If you keep lowering your dose, it'll work out," she told me, but I got worse. Everywhere I turned, I met "experts" who promised a salvation which never materialised. Their idea that I had to endure a long period of painful emotional turmoil, in order to come off lithium, put me in an unenviable position. It meant I tolerated being very ill for long periods of time; deeply depressed and psychotic, because I believed it was part of the healing process.

Two and a half years after I had started to lower my dose, I discovered an organisation which used high-grade supplements to feed the brain, whilst helping people to reduce their medication. When I discovered they had worked with over 100,000 people and I saw the amount of scientific research that existed to back up their claims; I was all in.

"Coming off meds isn't easy. You'll get withdrawals, but we can help you with that. You'll also go through a detox as your body gets rid of all the medication it has stored," one of the support staff told me in a scratchy voice. "About three months after you stop taking your meds, your body really starts detoxing; throwing off the lithium it has absorbed. The symptoms of your condition may return and you might have a relapse, but we can help you with that too. It can be tough and you've been on a high dose for a long time, but you can do it. If you can get through it, it's worth it." This organisation became my new lifeline as I continued to lower my dose.

The week after I took my final lithium pill, my body began to seriously detoxify. For a week, my urine became a dark brown, treacle-like fluid and for the next two years, I peed bubbles, as if I had drunk a bottle of washing up liquid. I was bedridden for six weeks with migraines, exhaustion, mouth ulcers, diarrhoea, blurred vision and extreme light sensitivity. I began to smell of petrol, curry, cigarettes and rotten eggs, which reminded me of my days in the Royal Edinburgh Hospital, when I had wandered around smelling of sulphur. I also became paranoid and depressed.

The process of lowering my lithium dose had now been going on for three years and I couldn't remember what it was like to be well. Every day was a fight, but the end of the tunnel was in sight. The support staff assured me all I had to do was to keep going and it would work out. My desperation to succeed blinkered my vision, like a racehorse galloping onwards on race day. I wouldn't change my mind; I was going to get off lithium no matter what.

There was good news. I would have days when I was symptom free, which gave me hope that the detox was coming to an end and encouraged me to keep going. After a few weeks off lithium, my chronic psoriasis healed, my muscle aches vanished and I was no longer craving water all the time. My sinuses functioned well and the tinnitus that had plagued me for years had gone. I even began to write and draw again! It was during this time I started to write books again: my first autobiographical book *The Broker who Broke Free* and then the novel *No Rest for the Wicked*.

What was even more remarkable was that I was thirty-eight-years old and began to feel my emotions for the first time since I had been nineteen. I cried and cried. My emotional life had been a desert for nearly twenty years, but I hadn't realised I had been thirsty. Now I could feel sadness, joy, melancholy, love and hope. It was startling. As these emotions arrived, the short temper which had plagued me since I began taking lithium disappeared. For the following two "lithium free" years, my wife and I didn't argue and I was no longer aggressive towards anyone. These positive signs spurred me on and provided evidence to support what I was doing. It was such a strange time. One day I would be ill enough to be in a mental hospital and the next I felt better than I had done for years.

As the weeks passed my mental health declined, but I wouldn't give in. I had invested three years and no matter how bad it got I wouldn't give up.

"You can do this Ollie. Any day the detox will be over and you'll feel like a new man," the support staff encouraged me.

That was when everything took a distinct turn for the worse. About three months after taking my last lithium pill,

I fell into the deepest psychosis I had ever experienced. It was the most extreme episode of my entire life. One moment I was lying in bed on an island in the Oslo Fjord, looking up at my wife as she stroked my head. The next I was being hunted across the Cosmos by alien assassins (see Chapter 1).

A few days later in Oslo, my psychosis took an even tighter grip. I now believed I was being held captive and that alien assassins were on their way to murder me in cold blood. Panicking, I sprinted into our sitting room and found my wife sitting on the sofa. Taking one look at her, I could tell she was in league with the aliens. So I ran towards her, letting out such a roar that she thought I was going to attack her. Instead, I sprinted straight past, tore open a window and shouted at the top of my lungs,

"Help! help! help!" Without wasting a second, I began to climb out of the window, determined to make my escape. My wife leapt up and grabbed one of my arms and a trouser leg, frantically trying to pull me back into the sitting room, but I wasn't having any of it. By now, I was halfway out of the window, about twenty feet above the solid concrete of the pavement below. Commuters stopped to watch the drama unfold as I strained to get to the ledge underneath me. The ledge was slippery and led nowhere, but – since I was the Messiah – I would be okay. My wife gave me another almighty tug, nearly pulling off my jeans, which were loose because I had lost so much weight. Somehow she managed to pull me back into the safety of our sitting room. If she had not had the strength and courage to rescue me, I have no doubt I would have broken my legs on the pavement below.

As quickly as it had arrived, the paranoid world of the hunted Messiah left me. Like a morning mist blown by a forgotten breeze, I returned to the reality that I shared with her. We ended up sitting on the sofa together, my wife holding my hand tightly, both of us shaken by what had transpired. The shock had pulled me back into myself and for a few minutes I experienced a tremendous feeling of love for her.

"What was that about?" we asked each other, managing to laugh nervously.

Then, without any warning, I shot up from the sofa and ran out of our front door. My wife gave chase and managed to get hold of me before I disappeared into the city.

When I first started lowering my medication, I wasn't entirely sure I was doing the right thing, so I became secretive. I didn't tell my parents what I was up to, as they had justifiable reasons to disagree with it and I was in no fit state to handle their worries or opposition. So I kept quiet. For a long time, we didn't involve my wife's family either, which meant we had little support around us when disaster struck. My wife was left to make most of the decisions on her own.

Back in the apartment, she locked the door and called the supplement support line. They told her my psychosis was due to a massive detoxification of lithium and if we persevered, it would end and all would be well. It never did. A group of friends took turns watching over me day and night, as I fell deeper and deeper into madness.

A few days passed and after many fruitless conversations with the supplement people, who didn't understand how serious my situation was, my wife contacted the local psychiatric unit. A nurse and a doctor came to see me at home that day. They were calm and kind, treating me with a great deal of sensitivity and respect. Before leaving, they gave my wife some antipsychotics meant for me. They wanted me to have the choice as to whether I took them or not.

Loyal to my wish to be medication free, which was also hers, my wife tried to keep the family afloat as we waited for the psychosis to lift. She knew how much it had cost me to get this far and believed the supplement people when they encouraged us to keep going. However, the time came when she decided enough was enough and gave me an antipsychotic pill. That same evening, I began to improve. No longer fighting to be medication free or afraid of what the doctors would say, I went into an Acute Psychiatric Unit in Oslo to get well. The antipsychotic steadily brought me back to the only dimension which mattered. This one.

Mission failed.

Learnings:

1. A wise psychiatrist is a good listener who knows they don't have all the answers.

2. Health professionals should be aware they may be afraid of a patient's desire to come off their medication. This is understandable because it can go badly wrong. However, a patients' concerns about side effects shouldn't be dismissed out of hand. They should be discussed. It may not be practical or even possible for some people to come off their medication, but pushing this desire under the table is unhelpful.

3. As soon as I stopped taking lithium, most of my side effects disappeared, my emotions returned and my irritability vanished. I also became far more unstable.

4. As I lowered my dose, the idea that I needed to "hang in there" no matter what, encouraged me to put up with

more suffering than I should have done.

5. The longer I had gone without lithium the harder it was for me to admit defeat and get back on it.

6. I hid what I was doing from my parents and other family members because I felt they wouldn't understand or agree with what I was doing. I also didn't want to cause them undue anxiety. My decision to be secretive was a mistake. It alienated my wife and I and put us under more pressure than we needed to be.

7. Even though the help offered from the supplement organisation didn't work for me, this doesn't take away from the fact that their supplement programme has and does help thousands of people with bipolar.

Chapter 12. Good people make all the difference

"You can't understand someone until you've walked for ten miles in their shoes."

– Anon.

I believe in being brave and not giving up too easily, but there comes a point when soldiering on becomes excessively stubborn. It is not necessarily easy to know when it is wise to push through resistance and when it is wise to give up, but every so often, it seems that *I* want to go one way and *life* wants to go another. In other words, I am fighting the natural flow of life. This is a spiritual way of looking at the world which I find helpful and may make sense to you.

I wanted to be medication free, but life didn't agree with me. So, it tried to set me on a different path, by making it increasingly difficult to go the way I was going. The longer I persisted with lowering lithium, the greater my suffering, but I didn't see the signs. I held onto my belief that I could be well without medication, so life squeezed me harder, hoping that eventually I would see sense.

Even after my spell in the Acute Psychiatric Unit in Oslo, I hadn't learned the valuable lesson of working with life rather than against it, but I was getting there. By this stage, I knew I needed psychiatric medication, but I was wary of going back on lithium. So began a year where my new psychiatrist and I tried to find the right medication for me. The antipsychotic I had been given by the acute team, which had ended my psychosis, had been very effective, but it had its downsides. It made me feel drowsy, I got ticks and twitches, felt down and had little energy. I don't think I laughed once whilst taking it, so it was not a good long term option. I then tried another medication which stopped my hallucinations in their tracks, but made me restless and dizzy and gave me a gnawing headache that never went away. So, I tried another, which didn't agree with me at all. It made me feel utterly numb, far more than lithium. I couldn't enjoy anything because I couldn't feel anything. It dealt with my depressive feelings, but left a void I couldn't live with.

Since stopping lithium, I had had such intense shakes and spasms I could have been mistaken for someone with Parkinson's disease. It got so bad, I once had to go to the Accident and Emergency ward because my neck had spasmed so violently I had problems breathing. Because of these spasms, my psychiatrist prescribed a medication which is used to treat Parkinson's disease. That didn't work either.

Somewhere along the way, I had developed a sensitivity to medication and no matter what I tried, they all disagreed with me. Health and stability continued to elude me, as I cycled from depression, to hypomania, with the occasional good day. As the year went on, my world shrank, as did my options. Nothing had worked for me. Not lithium, not alternative medicine; and now an array of conventional drugs didn't agree with me either. I thought I had ruined everything.

In this disillusioned state of mind, after years of trying to do it my way, finally the penny dropped. Enough was enough, I realised I had to stop imposing my will on this illness. I had to give in to life. I had to get more help. Part of giving up my fight came from my suffering wearing me down, part came from seeing the damage I had done and part came from total exhaustion. For the second time in my life, all I wanted was a bed in a safe, peaceful hospital, where I could give in to the doctors and nurses and let them heal me.

A few weeks after this decision, or perhaps because of it, my luck changed. Out of the blue, my psychiatrist sent me to a little hospital called Dr. Høst's Vei in the countryside outside Oslo. It was a gentle place, which gave its patients the opportunity to have a respite and try to find long term solutions to their mental problems. Dr. Høst's Vei was hidden away on top of a hill, surrounded by fir trees. It had an atmosphere which was calmer than any other mental hospital I had been in. The staff were friendly and laid back. I was given my own room and was able to go home at the weekends. It was here that I met a psychiatrist who had a profound impact on me.

Klaus Andresen was a sporty, energetic man in his late forties. He had a kind face which exuded confidence and intelligence. In our first meeting, I sat down on the edge of the chair he offered me, feeling nervous and vulnerable. Klaus listened to my story patiently, showing no surprise or disapproval at the choices I had made. Once I had finished talking, he told me something I had never expected to hear a psychiatrist say.

"I try all the medications I prescribe and lithium has the worst side effects of the lot. I understand why you tried to come off it, I really do."

I burst into tears. Finally, I had met a doctor who understood why I had done what I had done.

"I don't want to prescribe any medicine I haven't tried myself," he continued, "It doesn't seem fair to expect people to take a pill I know nothing about. So, I take each medication for a weekend and see how they affect me. I know it's only a weekend, but it gives me a taste of what the pills are like. Knowing a pill's side effects from the writing on the side of the box, is a long way away from living with those side effects."

Going against the medical establishment had created a heavier burden than I had appreciated. I had felt like a criminal, going against an institution I had been taught to trust. It had been a lonely, guilty decision which had ground me down. I regretted ever embarking on this idiotic journey. It had only led to suffering; for me, for my family and even for some of my friends.

Now one of the experts was telling me he understood why I had done what I had done and I can't begin to describe the relief. Finally, I had met a doctor who heard me out and treated my desire with respect. His approach rebuilt my trust in psychiatry and allowed me to let go of much of my guilt.

The doctors and nurses at Dr. Høst's Vei were unlike any I had experienced since Dr. Wrate. Instead of rushing to find a solution to my problems, they took time to discuss my concerns with me. They felt it was important that I felt my dilemma was being treated seriously. They didn't want me to feel forced into making big decisions before I was ready and put me under no pressure to go back on lithium, or any other type of medication. I had become accustomed to doctors telling me what to do, but the psychiatrists at Dr. Høst's Vei wanted to work in partnership with me and for us to find a solution together. Their approach gave me breathing space and allowed me to come to my own conclusions in my own time and it worked.

One day I knew. Going back on lithium was my best bet. It was a decision that brought some relief, but was overshadowed by a cutting disappointment. At the time, it seemed that all of the blood, sweat and tears had been in vain. All of the treatments, the losses and the mental agony had been for nothing. Not only was I mildly depressed, but I had so much regret to deal with. The life on lithium which lay ahead of me gave me no cause to celebrate. Yes, I would hopefully escape the serious episodes, but I would once again have to deal with the side effects. My hope of living an ordinary, healthy life had gone up in smoke.

When I began my quest, I had hoped I would end up healthier and happier. I had believed that a perfect solution to all of my health problems existed, but if it did, I hadn't found it. Four years of poor decisions and poor advice had taken me back to square one.

"I think it might be good if I went back on lithium," I told the doctors and they agreed.

That evening, two years to the day after I took what I thought was my last dose of lithium, I took my first dose of lithium. As I queued up to collect the pills from the nurse on the nightshift, I felt a mixture of unease and excitement. She handed me one of those thin, disposable, white plastic cups, which seem to inhabit every hospital the world over. I took it and stared at the two, chalky pills clinging to the bottom. Then I paused for what seemed like an uncomfortably long time, butterflies flapping madly in my stomach. Did I honestly want to go ahead with this?

A gulp of water and I had.

I nodded to the nurse and wandered off to bed.

Pulling the covers over my body, I lay down and closed my eyes; my mind acutely alert as I waited to see what would happen next. I had never been so attentive to what was going on inside my mind and body. I was like a cat sitting outside a mousehole, waiting for a glimpse of the mouse.

Sure enough, the ringing in my ears returned, as did the familiar feeling of my mouth becoming drier. Minutes later, the numbing, hardening sensation I knew so well enveloped my brain. It felt like molten metal was pouring into my head and setting fast, sealing off all escape routes for my errant emotions. The last two years without lithium, had allowed me to experience a rich variety of emotions, but this was now coming to an end. For a moment, I felt a sense of impending doom and then an acute terror, as I was smothered from the inside by this sensation. I was never going to feel any of those emotions again. I panicked and then prayed, sincerely hoping I was doing the right thing. Before I could contemplate this any further, I fell into a chemically hastened sleep, which didn't allow for dreams.

For the first weeks back on lithium, my depression refused to lift and I feared my life-saving medication no longer worked for me. Growing up isn't always easy, but in the months which followed, I grew up. It was a tough but necessary process for me. I went into a mental tunnel where I began to question everything; my spiritual path, my life choices and all of the ideas I had believed in. I regretted moving to Norway and losing close contact with my old friends and family. I regretted being a forty-year-old without a career and I regretted all the time I had lost. What had it all come to? I saw little meaning in anything and although I wasn't suicidal, I didn't particularly want to live. What was the point? I was going through a grieving process, but I was grieving for myself.

I didn't see it when I was in the midst of it all, but my dark tunnel eventually revealed the light. It helped me to get clear on my values and to get my priorities straight. What makes a man a good man? What was success to me? What did I stand for as a person? In many ways it was a mid-life crisis which came a few years earlier than expected.

With fortuitous timing, a breath of fresh air blew into my world, in the form of a psychologist called Tone Fagerli. Tone was a friendly, encouraging and competent therapist. A forty something woman with a practical, down to earth wisdom I related to. In my first meeting with her, her open smile and trustworthy air, put me at ease. Tone was very good at her job and after a few therapy sessions with her, I began to come out of the depression and see a way ahead. I had been consumed by bipolar for such a long time, but Tone helped me to take a step back and look at the illness with fresh eyes. She pointed out that, as someone who had bipolar, I had unrealistic expectations about what I could do and achieve. This had been true for me all of my life. I had set standards for myself (and others) which were unrealistically high. It was so helpful to hear this from an expert, which gave me permission to lower my standards and live a more balanced and relaxed life.

So, I put my more over-ambitious ideas to bed and gave myself some slack. I had a serious diagnosis and limitations came with that, there was no need to pile perfectionism on top of it all. Tone had a great sense of humour and reminded me to enjoy life with its simple pleasures, reassuring me that I could contribute to the world without having to conquer it. A life on lithium could be both rewarding and worthwhile. In short, she guided me out of the tunnel of my mid-life crisis and into a new and more hopeful state of mind.

By uncovering my inner confidence and getting clear on what my values were, living became easier because I could make decisions based on my values. I was no longer willing to compromise them and for the first time in my life, I felt I was in charge of my own destiny.

When I first started taking lithium, I had developed a habit of asking too many people for advice. Whenever I faced decisions, I turned to others, because I didn't trust myself. In general, I believe seeking advice is wise, but I took it too far. I put too much weight on what others thought, instead of looking inside myself for the answers. Now I was committed to listening to my own inner wisdom. It was time to trust myself, follow my own values and try to build a life that was supportive and meaningful.

As my strength returned, it became clear that somewhere along the way, I had overcome my fear of making mistakes. I began to see life as more of a game rather than a battle. I became better at handling responsibility, but at the same time I took myself less seriously. Tone helped me to see that although the process of coming off medication had been tough; I had learned some valuable lessons about who I was and who I wasn't. I had also got clear on what was most important to me.

In an attempt to reduce the side effects, the doctors at Dr. Høst's Vei had agreed that I could try to find the lowest dose of lithium which would keep me stable. By experimenting, I found I could manage on a lower level than before. This dose, which I am on to this day, keeps my blood levels around the lower end of the therapeutic range (sometimes within it, sometimes a little below). It doesn't give me quite as much mental stability as my original dose, but it gives me enough and my side effects are far easier to handle. This new level has transformed my life.

My head is now clearer, my brain functions better and I can read books again. My hallucinations have all but disappeared and I don't get lost within two hundred metres of my flat. I also have more mental energy and zest for life. Had I not found stability on this lower level, I would not have been able to write this book.

I continue to have most of the physical side effects I had on the higher dose of lithium, such as stiff muscles and exhaustion, but they are less intense. My tremors have stopped. The only side effect which is worse on the lower does are the headaches I now get, but I can live with these.

The fear that I would once again be robbed of an emotional life, hasn't come to fruition. I sometimes feel jealous or sad and although my irritability has returned, it isn't as ferocious. Now I can actually feel the anger behind it, but be aware enough to refrain from arguing with my wife or anyone else. It is exciting to live a life that includes emotions. Joy, contentment, peace, anger and love are now part of my life. I'm the only person I know who is enthusiastic about my ability to feel anger! My emotions might not be as intense as they were before I ever began lithium, but it is amazing to feel them.

Learnings:

1. Experimenting with medications was extraordinarily challenging for me.

2. To meet a psychiatrist who heard me out and understood my choices, allayed a great deal of my guilt and restored my trust in the medical establishment.

3. Finding stability on a lower dose of lithium has improved my standard of living significantly.

4. The high level of respect and autonomy I was given in Dr. Høst's Vei, helped me to take a balanced look at bipolar. They never put me under pressure to take medication, which ironically made it easier to for me to go back on lithium.

Chapter 13. Acceptance: the key to recovery

"What doesn't kill you makes you stronger."

– Old proverb.

It may sound odd, that nearly twenty-five years after my initial diagnosis, I had not fully accepted that I suffered from bipolar; but after waking up in the Acute Psychiatric Unit in Oslo at the age of forty I finally found myself thinking,

"I have a mental illness. I need to start looking after myself."

In life there are countless situations which can't be controlled and many problems which can't be solved. Part of maturing as an adult is facing up to this fact and accepting it. Acceptance is not a concept which is talked about enough, which is a shame because it is a key to living a fulfilling life. So, what exactly is acceptance? In my view it is learning to cooperate with life the way it is, rather than struggling to change it when I can't. It is learning to be okay with not getting it all my own way.

Acceptance is not the same as resignation. Resignation is passive and feels helpless. Resignation gives up easily and can lead to resentment, whereas acceptance is active and empowering. If I accept a situation, I have more energy to change it if I can. If I resign myself to a situation, I can't be bothered to try to change it. Resignation says,

"I don't like this, but I have to put up with it."

Acceptance says,

"I will change this if I can, but if I can't, I will make the most of it."

After my first episode, I wasn't close to coming to terms with having a mental illness. I accepted bipolar to the degree that I was willing to take lithium every day, but that was as far as it went. I didn't make any attempts to educate myself about the illness or join any support groups, nor did I adopt useful boundaries to support my mental health. I was young and not ready to accept the gravity of my situation. I decided I had dealt with bipolar and believing this fairy tale, I shut it out and ploughed on with life, rarely allowing myself to think about what I had been through. In my own mind, I had dealt with the illness and believed if I kept taking my pills everything would be fine. If I did talk about the condition, it was from the perspective that I had heroically overcome an illness which would have defeated normal people. I was far from humble.

I think my "head in the sand" reaction was natural for a young man who had gone through a lot and not yet come to terms with what had happened. Had I been wiser, I would have taken some time to learn about bipolar and create a life which supported my mental health, but I wasn't. So I lived in denial; drinking, partying, eating badly and doing whatever foolish things I felt like doing. In my twenties, my mother gave me a book about bipolar and I didn't even bother to open it. Why would I? Why dwell on an illness I had already conquered?

Deep down, I was scared. My first episode had bolted shut doors in my mind which I didn't dare to open for fear of what I might find. If I read about bipolar, I might learn something I would rather not know. Perhaps my life expectancy would be shorter? [22] Or I could become ill even though I was taking lithium? Ignorance seemed safer.

Growing up, I was taught the route to happiness was through success. Success would give me both money and choice, which would deliver happiness. Bipolar threatened this dream. It reduced my choices, limited the ways I could make money and robbed me of my happiness. How could I accept such an illness?

Deep down, I knew something was wrong with my brain, but if I dared to accept I had an incurable, life-long diagnosis, I would have felt vulnerable and weak. As a young man I *had* to feel strong even if I wasn't. I had ambitions and wanted to leave my mark on the world. As far as I was concerned, acknowledging my weaknesses was not going to help me to reach my goals. Had I accepted bipolar with a level of maturity, which at the time was beyond me, I would have looked for a career which supported my health rather than challenged it. One that offered me stability and didn't aggravate the condition. Instead, I got a job on the trading floor of an investment bank. Not exactly a peaceful place to be.

Back then, if you had asked me if I had accepted having bipolar, I would have replied overconfidently,

"Yeah. Of course, I've accepted it," because I thought I had. I wasn't embarrassed to tell people about my condition, so I must have accepted it. I was proud I had been into the pit of despair and had bounced back; and I wore my suffering like a badge of honour. I believed I was special because I had visited the depths of hell and had become a deeper and more interesting person because of it. From one perspective this was true, but it was far from the whole story.

In my forties, after four years of struggling to be lithium free, my massive detox and psychosis, finally forced me to face the elephant in the corner of the room. Accepting this mental reality which had been staring me in the face since I was seventeen, was no walk in the park. It had taken over twenty years for me to get to that place. There were several stages in this evolution of acceptance, all of which are discussed below:

1. Resistance is futile:

When we humans are presented with situations that seem to threaten our idea of how the world should be, resistance tends to be our go-to reaction. The more unfair or wrong we believe a situation is, the harder we resist it. Resistance can be as simple as complaining about the weather, hating rush hour traffic, or refusing to accept we are tired and need a rest. Every day we resist a multitude of minor irritations, but whenever we do this, we are picking a fight with life and when we pick a fight with life, there is only going to be one winner. Resistance clouds our perception and shrinks our options. It focuses our mind on negativity rather than solutions. Small resistances can be irritating, but when we resist a meaningful part of our life things can go awry.

Before I could begin to relate to bipolar in a realistic way, I had to stop resisting it. Initially I resisted having the illness. Then I resisted changing my lifestyle to support my mental health. Years later, I resisted having to take lithium. Finally, I resisted going back on it.

At each step of the way, my suffering was compounded by my resistance to what was happening or what was clearly meant to happen. After I stopped resisting bipolar and the limitations which came with it, I no longer saw it as an enemy and I was able to get on with finding solutions.

2. Giving up the fight:

I have found it hard to accept the physical discomfort that comes with lithium and I have spent a lot of energy fighting the side effects. A few years ago, there came a moment when I had been mentally well, but physically sick for months and it finally dawned on me:

"I might never get better. I might be ill for the rest of my life," I thought to myself, but instead of being angry or sad, I began to chuckle.

"What's so funny?" my wife asked, curious as to why her husband was giggling to himself.

"I'm a wreck, but it's okay. I'm happy."

This realisation was a turning point for me. Realising my mental stability and happiness were more important than my physical health or life circumstances, was a transformative discovery. Accepting I might never feel strong and healthy again and being okay with this possibility, removed the self-imposed pressure of consistently struggling to get well. I had done my best to find a solution to my health problems and it had partially worked, could I not be satisfied with that? Once I stopped fighting the side effects an ease flooded into my mind. The energy I had spent in my battle to get well was now freed up for better things, like appreciating what I had rather than fighting to improve my health.

In society we often talk about fighting our problems. We fight cancer, crime and mental illness, but I don't like this approach. I would rather find peace with my problems because peace is more powerful. Fighting sets me up against an enemy which has to be defeated. It creates friction and stress. Acceptance on the other hand, puts me in a relaxed, open state from which I can approach my problems in a more pragmatic and creative way. The wise Tai Chi Master, who yields to overcome, has greater long term success than the boxer who tries to batter his opponent into submission every time he steps into the ring. Whether I like it or not, bipolar is a part of me and I have no desire to be at war with any part of myself.

When it comes to curing an illness, accepting it is one of the last things most people think of doing. It seems counterintuitive. Yet, when I stopped fighting and accepted that I might never get well, opportunities to improve my health appeared out of nowhere. Within two weeks, my health started to get better, due to the small miracles that had come to me. I was offered free treatments by a gifted healer, I discovered that electrolytes took some of my headaches away and out of the blue, I was offered a part time job. I firmly believe my decision to "accept" rather than "battle" bipolar attracted new opportunities. Had I continued fighting to get well, I doubt these opportunities would have appeared and if they had, I would probably not have taken advantage of them.

3. Letting go of regrets:

When we are young, we dream about the incredible things we are going to do with our life. Fast forward thirty years and life has usually panned out quite differently. There often comes a time when we look back and compare our dreams to reality and we don't like what we see.

When I recovered from my last episode, I took a long, hard look at myself. Had I lived the life I had wanted to? Had I channelled my efforts into the right areas? The answer was sometimes "yes," but sometimes "no." I was hounded by regrets and I blamed myself and others for my failures. I regretted my choices and resented people for giving me bad advice or not standing by me when things got rough. Life hadn't turned out even close to what I had hoped for and this made me feel sad and disappointed.

This was the final piece of my acceptance puzzle, accepting that life hadn't panned out the way I had wanted it to. Once I did this, my failures became my teachers and my perspective changed. Although I hadn't had the conventional success I had desired, good things had come from my "failure." I was happier and wiser thanks to my challenges and even following bad advice from those I had trusted, had taught me valuable lessons. I realised by holding grudges, I was only punishing myself and that hanging onto regrets was a waste of time. Regrets are a normal part of life, but it was time for me to let them go and move on. When I did, the beauty of my life, as it was, became more apparent.

It is important to know that at no point could I have forced myself to accept bipolar. I had to be ready to do it. My words are not meant to push anyone into forcing themselves to accept their lot. There is a time and a place for everything.

Chapter 14. Balance: Finding a middle way

"Our task is to strike a balance, to find a middle way and learn not to overextend ourselves with extraneous activities and preoccupations, but to simplify our lives… The key to finding a happy balance in modern life is simplicity."

– Sogyal Rimpoche.

Once I was on a lower dose of lithium and had accepted that being bipolar had consequences, which I needed to address, it became easier to look at the illness objectively. This enabled to me to tap into a resource that had been hidden from me for large parts of my adult life: common sense. It may sound bizarre, but after such a long estrangement, it was uncommonly liberating for common sense to be a part of my decision-making process.

I saw I needed to create a balanced life which was supportive of my mental health and the days of doing exactly what I wanted, without considering the consequences, were over. In my younger days, I got away with living an unbalanced life, but now I couldn't. I had to acknowledge not only my dreams and desires, but also the limitations bipolar imposed upon me. This meant balancing what I wanted with what was possible.

Fortunately, those years of imbalance were not entirely wasted, because they helped me to discover what didn't work. Through trial and error, I have now adopted certain approaches that have improved my experience of a life with bipolar. I have amassed an array of approaches to support and strengthen my mental health. These have helped me to build a more balanced life and are listed below: Please be aware that none of these approaches are recommendations. They are merely approaches which have helped me. I am not qualified to give any advice on mental health, merely to share what I have experienced. It is always wise to consult your doctor or psychiatrist before trying anything that might affect your mental state. Something which works for me, may not work, for someone else, and may even be detrimental.

1. Medication: I need to take lithium on a long term basis and roughly once a year I need antipsychotics to prevent a psychosis from manifesting. Other bipolar sufferers might only need medication for shorter periods and some not at all. I know of people who manage this illness without medication, but that option hasn't worked for me.

I find great comfort in knowing that if I get symptoms of psychosis or mania, I can do something about them. Being able to knock a potential episode on the head gives me a sense of security and control. It also means I can avoid the suffering of an episode and the struggle of the aftermath, which can take over a year out of my life.

Sometimes, when I put lithium or antipsychotic pills into the palm of my hand, I thank them for keeping me sane before swallowing them. It is a minor action, but it feels good to remind myself that these pills are keeping me well. It also steers my mind away from negative thoughts about medication.

2. Psychotherapy: It was important for me to have a competent professional who I trusted and could talk with. Before Tone, my other psychologists were cold fish who didn't seem to be happy. If I don't consider a psychologist to be happy, I don't rate their chances of helping me get there.

I believed I could think my way through my own problems, but when I worked with Tone, we came up with far better solutions than I could have done alone. Having a good psychologist also took the pressure off my wife, who had become my sounding board and emotional crutch. The resentment I experienced after my final episode could have chewed me up for years. My therapy with Tone helped me to contextualise what had happened, let go of my feelings of resentment and move on.

3. Action: Being occupied with a project I enjoy gives me energy and stops me from feeling down. It diverts my attention away from my problems, into other more useful avenues. Whether it is writing a book, making videos, or installing a new washing machine, I'm happier when I'm busy. The key for me is to find a healthy balance between doing and relaxing. It doesn't work if I am running around like a mad march hare, trying to avoid the negative thoughts in my head. I need down time watching movies, going for walks and chatting in coffee shops. However, having projects, learning something new, setting myself a goal or going on an adventure, all give me good reasons to get out of bed in the morning.

From what I have seen, mental hospitals would be more effective if the patients had more to do. Even in Dr. Høst's Vei, which I consider to be a cutting-edge hospital, most of my day was spent doing nothing. Apart from a daily discussion group, the odd art class and a one hour a week gym session, not much happened. My impression of mental hospitals is that the patients are there to keep them safe, whilst they wait for the medication to work. I would like to see a more proactive healing approach. This means not just keeping patients in a ward until they function well enough to go home, but giving them a kick start in the healing process whilst still in hospital.

I needed action to pull me out of my depression faster and there was a distinct lack of it, particularly physical action. It would have been good to have done some gardening, dancing, singing or to have gone for a group run in the woods. A game of five-a-side football would have been fantastic. Anything to instill a bit of energy or purpose. I realise the resources are not necessarily there to organise these activities and the patients don't necessarily have the energy or capacity to do them, but I still feel it would make a big difference where possible.

4. Getting out of my comfort zone: In the West we can be comfortable for long periods of our life, but this isn't necessarily good for us. Too many hours in front of a screen, too much time spent indoors and too little variation isn't good for our souls. I relish the times when I can go ice bathing in the sea, wild swimming in rivers, walking in the heavy rain or riding my motorbike, because these activities bring out my zest for life.

There is evidence that ice bathing can not only prevent, but also treat depression and this is my personal experience. When I swim in freezing seawater on a winter's day in Norway, I feel calm, present and alive for many days after. It picks up my mood and at the same time calms me. A study by the British Medical Journal Case Report, discovered that weekly cold water swims led to an immediate improvement in mood following each swim and a sustained and gradual reduction in the symptoms of depression. [23]

Knowing I have done something wild and exciting and not just stared at a computer screen all day is good for my mental state. Nature has a presence and a peace which makes me feel alive. Even if it isn't as dynamic as leaping into the sea, simply getting out in nature is good for me. When I ride my motorbike, I have to be alert and therefore present. There is no time for me to dwell on my problems and it makes me feel exhilarated.

5. Humour: My ability to laugh at myself has been a lifesaver. In a world where taking ourselves too seriously is all too tempting and often encouraged, a healthy dose of humour and self-irony goes a long way.

There are few things too inappropriate, rude or embarrassing for me to have a laugh about, including my own mental issues. Those people who work with the toughest parts of life; the doctors, nurses, paramedics, fire brigade and the military, often have the darkest sense of humour. They know the important role laughter plays in de-stressing and de-escalating stressful situations. They would rather have a good laugh and get on with saving lives, than take themselves too seriously.

No one wants to go through tough times, but they are easier to bear if we can laugh at ourselves. Humour takes the edge off our problems by recontextualising them. We see this most clearly with the comedians who make us laugh at ourselves and our strange habits. Laughter is not necessarily the best medicine, but it is right up there.

I want to give a message of hope and have a good laugh along the way. Spending time with humorous, uplifting people and watching plenty of comedy shows, is now a part of my routine and puts a smile on my face. From time to time, life goes a bit wonky and I am far from perfect. I am not the most disciplined person in the world and I don't always manage to follow my "live better with bipolar" points consistently. But that is life and when I don't, the best approach is for me to laugh.

6. Giving to others: The happiest people I know are those who find ways to give to others. When one talks about giving, the emphasis tends to be on how the receiver benefits, but the act of giving benefits the giver too. When I give, it may look like I am losing something because I am, quite literally, giving something away. But what goes around comes around and my generosity comes back to me. Some people are not good at receiving and that's okay, I never force my help on anyone.

When I give, I tend to forget about my worries. It is hard for me to focus on my problems whilst helping someone else. Giving shows me I can make a difference. It lifts me up, it creates connection and it can heal conflicts.

How I express my generosity is up to me. It can be giving time, money, a shoulder to cry on, or a myriad of other things. Giving can feel natural, but if you are not in the habit of doing so, it can seem awkward. If your family or friends haven't shown you how to give, then you may need to teach yourself. How do you do this? You take a deep breath and start giving.

7. Purpose: I spent years worrying about finding my life's purpose, unsure if I ever would. I thought it had to be grand and impressive, but this isn't necessary. Some people find their one significant purpose, some don't. A lot of this seems to come down to luck.

I find it equally rewarding to instill purpose into parts of my everyday life that most people would call mundane. Purpose is malleable and although some things do give my life a greater meaning, the simple things can install a sense of meaning too. I can fill almost any task I do with purpose if I choose to. Instead of grumbling about doing the washing up, I can see it as a service to my family. Instead of moaning about the litter on the street, I can pick it up and improve my neighbourhood.

So, rather than worrying about finding your life purpose, which you may never do, give the small things in your life purpose and see what happens.

8. Sleep: Whilst in my first year of university, I went on holiday to Greece with a great friend. I booked cheap flights that left late in the evening and we arrived in a deserted airport at three o'clock in the morning. I missed out on one night's sleep and the following day I began to have panic attacks. My fear that I was going to get ill again, compounded by the lack of sleep, meant I ended up flying home, the holiday ruined.

It is well known that sleep is good for mental health and is particularly important for people with bipolar. [24] However, knowing it is good to sleep and being able to sleep are two entirely different things. The internal pressure of knowing I need to sleep, but not being able to, can itself lead to sleepless nights.

On a high dose of lithium, I slept deeply for nine or ten hours a night, but now my sleep is light and fragmented. In my quest for better sleep, I have tried a variety of approaches and the ones that have had a positive effect for me are: CBD oil, meditation, homeopathy, hot milk, eating less sugar, giving up caffeine, exercise, breathing exercises, sedatives, going to bed at a reasonable hour, reducing screen time and reducing the blue light from screens. [25]

I still can't control whether I sleep or not, but I can control my attitude towards it. I am now fairly relaxed about my sleep patterns and if I am awake at three o'clock in the morning, I take a sleeping pill, which usually knocks me out. I do this to stop myself worrying about going into a psychosis that can come from a lack of sleep. Now, when I travel, I ask for a quiet room or I pay a bit more for flights which leave at a reasonable time of day. I do whatever I can to protect my sleep.

9. Identification and awareness: A human being's attention is a powerful creative tool. What I focus on grows, which means the more I think and talk about bipolar, the more the whole illness grows in my awareness. This means I start to identify more strongly with being bipolar than I need to. Some people identify with their mental illness so strongly, they carry it around with them wherever they go, eager to discuss it or complain about it whenever they get the chance.

I try to keep a healthy emotional distance from bipolar, rather than being consumed by it. There are more interesting things to talk about than my illness. I don't ignore bipolar completely, I do what I need to do to stay well, but the less I identify with it, the freer I am to get on with life.

Bipolar is an illness which can be managed; and managing it often becomes easier over time. [26] I sometimes listen to bipolar podcasts or read the odd book or article on the subject. Occasionally I look at reputable websites or journals too, but I don't want to spend too much time being absorbed in bipolar. It is a balance between educating myself about my illness and getting on with living.

In writing this book, I had to identify with bipolar more than I have done for years, but surprisingly it hasn't consumed me. I believe this to be so because I am not too strongly attached to it. I have the illness, but I am not the illness.

10. Friendships: Friendships are important to me and a huge bonus to my mental health. I am a sociable person and spending time with good people sparks me up. If I'm in a funk, spending time with a good friend is one of the best ways to get me to a better place.

My episodes have challenged my friendships because as soon as my laughter was replaced with depression, many of the people I thought were friends vanished. The other side of the coin was I was shown genuine friendship from some unexpected sources. What I learned from this is to make a point of being proactive with most of my friendships. I also now know how important it is to make an effort and reach out to friends who are in trouble. The qualities I want from a friendship, I try to give to it. I have done my fair share of letting friends down; sometimes due to bipolar and sometimes because I was thoughtless or selfish, but I do my best to make things right when I can. Friendships and close relationships are particularly valuable to the mentally ill, so investing time and energy in them is wise.

If you are a friend to someone with a mental illness, know you are important. Mental illness can be tough to handle and sometimes it's hard to be around. It can be confusing to know what to do and it is normal to think you are interfering or doing something wrong. Sometimes communication is welcomed by the patient, at other times the patient may not want any contact at all. Sometimes they may want it, but be too ill to communicate this. If in doubt, I think it is usually better to take the risk and show that you care. Good friends are often the ones who dare to interfere.

As a friend of someone who is mentally ill, it can be helpful to see your friend as someone who is possessed by an illness. When ill, they are not themselves and probably don't mean many of the strange or hurtful things they may say. The traits you know and love may not be there, but this is the illness you see, not them. The person behind the illness still needs you. More than ever.

11. Stress management: It isn't possible to escape all forms of stress and neither is it desirable. A bit of stress from time to time is part of being a human. It can spark me up, build resilience and motivate me to succeed. However, chronic stress or stress which is overwhelming, is not good for me. If I take on too many tasks or over commit, I easily become overwhelmed. By being aware of what supports my health, versus what undermines it, I can reduce the amount of stress I experience.

My tendency is to be over-optimistic about how much I can do and I sometimes let people down because I have too much on my plate. Because of this, I have learned to schedule a rest day after a busy day. I limit the number of appointments I have in one day and I take plenty of breaks. Because I am generally open about having bipolar, I can warn people that I'm not always reliable, which takes the pressure off and supports the relationship. Sometimes it is wise to be honest about my situation and sometimes it is better to keep quiet, depending on whom I'm dealing with. Some people are sympathetic and others quite the opposite. It isn't always easy to tell how a person will react to discovering that I have a mental illness.

Having plenty of alone time also reduces my stress levels. It isn't good for me to have too many things to focus on at once and I thrive when I can devote myself fully to one project at a time.

Meditation is my most effective tool to reduce stress. I meditate every day which releases tension and makes me more relaxed. From time to time, I have to let off steam. On rare occasions, I stay up late at night or get drunk with friends. I pay the price with a hangover, like anyone else, but it does my spirit good. It's no fun to be well behaved all the time.

12. Gratitude: I used to like moaning. It was a way of bonding with people over our mutual dissatisfactions.

However, it spread negativity and did nothing for my mood. One day I made the conscious decision to change this habit and to be more grateful for what I have. Why not look for the good? There is a hell of a lot of it out there.

By being grateful for the feeling of fresh air in my lungs and the food I eat, an otherwise bleak day can transform into a good one. If I focus on what's wrong, I strengthen those pathways in my brain and my tendency to be negative increases. A negative brain sees and experiences more negativity. That is not what I need! Instead, I have made it a habit of expressing my gratitude whenever I can. I thank shopkeepers and bus drivers for their service and I thank my friends and family for being amazing. It makes me and them feel better.

13. Avoiding negativity: I don't think watching a lot of news is particularly good for anyone's mental health. When I was a patient in the Royal Edinburgh Hospital, I was rocked by a negative news story. It was most unexpected. I was watching the news in ward one, when an awful image appeared on the screen. It was footage of the pilot of an American Black Hawk helicopter which had been shot down in Somalia. The pilot was slouched against a wall, his face cut and one of his eyes black, looking frightened. The news then cut to a dead, half-naked American soldier, being dragged through the streets by a rope strapped to his ankle. I was vulnerable at that time and these images horrified me. I was convinced the end of the world was unfolding in front of my eyes and for months afterwards I had flashbacks.

The majority of news channels focus on the most negative and dramatic stories they can find and don't give a balanced picture of what is truly going on in the world. I limit the amount of news I see and try to be discerning about what sources I use. Instead of the tabloids, broadsheets and mainstream news channels, I follow two sources of positive news. [27] I avoid watching horror movies or very violent movies and try to steer clear of negative conversations when I can.

The mental hospitals I have been in could benefit from promoting more positivity. I have attended too many meetings where patients talked solely about their problems and the general focus was negative. Whilst it is necessary to discuss heavy topics from time to time, moving discussions towards solutions would have been beneficial in those meetings. Discussing what we hoped to do when we were well, or talking about what we appreciated in our lives, would have helped to balance the negativity those sessions sometimes created.

14. Exercise: You may wonder why I haven't written about exercise, as it is widely known to support mental health. This is because of the way I react to lithium. If I overdo exercise, I get a migraine and a three-day hang over. My personality changes and I become more aggressive, argumentative and opinionated, so I have had to give up most forms of exercise. I have yet to understand why this happens.

I love playing sport and my inability to do so is one of my biggest disappointments. I still use my body as much as I can. I go for gentle walks, swim in nature, do some stretches in the morning and practice Tai Chi.

15. Financial support: The financial support I have received from the Norwegian State, has made my process of recovery and stabilisation significantly easier.

I am paid a fixed amount every month and on top of this, I am allowed to earn some extra money for myself. If earn above a certain limit, my monthly allowance is gradually reduced, but my right to receive my benefits isn't taken away. This system is ingenious because it gives me a safety net and also an incentive to work. If I am well enough, I can work. If I am not, I don't starve.

Knowing there is financial help available, when I need it, greatly reduces the stress of having bipolar. I am aware this is not the situation in most countries, but I am mentioning it here because I want to spread the word about this excellent system. I believe people should have a safety net and also have an incentive to work if they can.

16. Asking for help: When I was ill it was common to find myself trying to handle my problems on my own. I felt responsible for sorting myself out and wasn't used to asking for help. I imagined other people were too busy to help, or I felt embarrassed about needing help. This felt lonely and difficult, but help was usually close at hand whenever I asked for it.

Sometimes help arrived unasked, but more often than not, I had to step forward, admit my "weakness" and ask for it. This sometimes felt awkward and took a certain amount of courage and humility to do. Yet, it was vital. No man or woman is an island and it was never worth pretending to be one. I discovered a surprising number of people are happy to help when asked.

17. Meditation: The meditation I have practised for the last twenty years is called Ascension. It has been a very significant part of me finding peace with bipolar. This meditation taught me to create a distance to my thoughts, which means I can now watch them instead of being consumed by them. I have developed an insight into my mind and therefore my illness, that is uncommon. Psychiatrists and psychologists who I have met have been surprised at my level of self-awareness and ability to spot an approaching episode. They are also surprised at how much insight I have into bipolar, much of which I can thank meditation for.

If one suffers from a mental illness, it is wise to be cautious when it comes to meditation, as it can be counterproductive. There are many types on offer; some are excellent and others are far from it. I consider the meditation I do to be excellent. This is because it focuses on allowing experiences to happen, rather than trying to suppress or control them. There is no need to attempt to silence the mind or stop thoughts or emotions, which I find beneficial. It can also be practiced gently and with my eyes open.

If I meditate for too long it can destabilise me. I can get angry and more restless rather than peaceful. Meditating when depressed isn't good for me either. One of the last things I should be doing when I'm down, is going into myself and focusing on my mind.

For a mentally stable person, meditation tends to have a calming effect because it activates the parasympathetic nervous system, which is responsible for rest. However, a depressed person's nervous system doesn't need more calming down, if anything it probably needs stimulation. [28] I know of one case where a man with bipolar learned to meditate when he was unstable and he became psychotic. So, I believe caution is a very good idea.

Meditation can occasionally bring up old traumas, which can't necessarily be resolved through meditation alone. Most often this is not the case, but issues with trauma are more likely to happen for mentally unstable people. In such cases, additional help, such as professional counselling, therapy or even medication may be needed.

If someone with a mental illness wants to learn how to meditate I always encourage them to:

1. Consult their doctor first.

2. Only learn when they have been well and stable for at least six months.

3. Start very slowly and with support.

4. Tell their meditation teacher they have mental challenges.

In the following chapter I write more about my meditation practice.

Chapter 15. Meditation: Finding the presence within

"The present moment is filled with joy and happiness. If you are attentive, you will see it."

– Thich Nhat Hanh, Buddhist monk.

At the time of writing this book, I have been taking a lower dose of lithium for over five years, with a great deal of success. Because lithium provides a stable mental platform, I am able to reap the rewards of twenty years of meditation practice. Without this drug, my brain doesn't function well enough for meditation to work. I need a strong foundation in order to build a house.

In 2002, when I learned to meditate, I wasn't a particularly happy guy. I wasn't completely miserable either, but I was struggling. Trying to cope with the external pressures of life and the internal pressures of my bipolar mind was far from straightforward. I tried to look confident and act like I had got it all together, but the truth was far from it. I was so fast I never gave myself time to reflect, pushing myself onwards at the behest of my hurried mind. I pushed myself to get good grades at school, I pushed myself to be a great sales trader, I was always pushing myself to be good at something. As soon as I achieved one goal, another would appear and then another and another. Like a hamster on a wheel, I kept running, driven onwards by the endless barrage of thoughts which ran around my head.

Before I learned to meditate, I had a tormented mind, full of fearful and argumentative thoughts. It would sometimes scream at me for weeks on end, as if it wanted to destroy me. I got used to it, in the same way we all get used to things which won't go away. However, meditation offered me a way to distance myself from my mind. It enabled me to find a level of peace, contentment and happiness that is rare in this modern world, even amongst people who have no mental issues. Now my mind is, for the most part, tranquil and peaceful. It is a safe place to be. My negative thoughts have virtually stopped. I smile and laugh easily, but it isn't the laughter of mania. I feel a deep peace and contentment, but it isn't the sluggishness of depression.

Ascension [29] has helped me enormously and has been a key factor in my befriending of bipolar. It has done so much for me I could write pages and pages on its benefits. It has freed me from negative thoughts and thinking, given me an inner balance and improved my decision making. It has developed patience, compassion, inner strength and my ability to function well in relationships.

These days, I am fortunate because I don't get carried away with the typical worries a bipolar sufferer might have. Due to my meditation training, which is twenty years long, I don't spend much time worrying about the negative effects my medication may be having on my kidneys and liver, that my memory is remarkably bad, or that I could have a relapse at any time. Not worrying keeps me calm which makes it easier for me to stay well and take the necessary actions to prevent a relapse. It also makes my life more fun and alive.

Meditation works by making me more aware of two things:

1. The thoughts in my mind. The average person has between twelve and sixty thousand thoughts a day. Of those, 80% are negative and 95% are the same repetitive thoughts as the day before. [30] My thoughts pull my attention away from the present moment, causing me to doubt, feel negative, confused or stressed. Of course, some thoughts are positive and creative, but these tend to be in the minority. By giving less attention to my thoughts, I experience less stress and suffering. I don't worry, over analyse, regret or fear the future. My attention is freed to live in the present moment, and the present moment is great.

2. An inner presence of awareness or peace. By putting more of my attention on this state, I'm filled with more calm and inner stability. This presence is the corner stone of many Eastern mystical traditions, but has been largely forgotten in the West. In the last decade or two, an interest in experiencing the presence within has been re-ignited in Western society. This presence can't be seen or scientifically measured; it can only be experienced, and whenever I am experiencing it, I am at peace. As natural as this state is, it is still unknown to most westerners, partly because it is so subtle it can be easily missed. This presence exists right under our nose, yet the busyness of life and our habit of almost constantly thinking, can take up all our attention, leaving nothing left to be aware.

You were probably never taught about presence at school and your parents probably didn't know about it either. So, although people have been exploring this state for thousands of years, to most in the modern world, it is a new phenomenon.

If you remember any of the happiest moments of your life, you'll see you were present during them. You weren't thinking about other things, you were absolutely attentive to what was happening in front of you. Whether you were looking into your newborn's eyes or hitting your greatest golf shot, you were present and the heating bill never came into your mind.

My journey from suffering to peace, began because I knew I couldn't find true happiness in a career, a relationship, or material success. Of course, supportive life circumstances can help, but lasting happiness is found within.

I knew I needed help and it arrived the weekend I learned to meditate in Glastonbury. When I learned I knew nothing about the presence, but after a few months of meditating, I discovered what it was. I then put my efforts into cultivating a relationship with it. Over time, it became easier and easier to find it and now it is my normal state.

The more I tapped into it, the better my experience of life became; not necessarily in obvious ways, like being showered with gifts or getting exactly what I wanted, but in subtler ones. I became more in tune with who I am and began to enjoy my own company more. I used to be plagued by regrets about my past and a fear of what might happen to me in the future, but through meditation I have managed to let go of my worries. I have learned to see life as it is, rather than how my thoughts tell me it is. From being a guy struggling with the challenges of bipolar, I am now someone who isn't so shaken by the ups and downs of life or my illness. I wake up most mornings feeling happy. It has taken dedication, patience, time and practice, but it has been worth it.

Whenever I have been beset by an episode, I have had to put my meditation journey on hold. It is not advisable to meditate when I'm mentally ill, but when I'm well again, I can return to my path. I am convinced that being present has unlocked the key to me becoming a happy human being. I also feel it is important to mention that the therapy I received complemented my meditation practice. It enabled me to understand my problems and recontextualise or solve them. Life still throws challenges at me and bipolar is not always plain sailing, but I'm far better equipped to deal with them now.

Chapter 16. Befriending bipolar

"Everything can be taken from a man, but one thing, the last of the human freedoms. To choose one's attitude in any given set of circumstances. To choose one's own way."

– Victor Frankl, author.

Bipolar can bless people with creativity, intelligence, charm, sensitivity and a way of seeing the world which is out of the box. Throughout history, many talented individuals may not have possessed their genius without this illness. Vincent Van Gogh, Ludwig van Beethoven, Wolfgang Amadeus Mozart, Frank Sinatra, Virginia Woolf, Winston Churchill and Isaac Newton were all diagnosed with, or suspected of having, manic depression (bipolar). The world would be a much poorer place without them.

Bipolar is always with me, lurking in the background and influencing my life in subtle and not so subtle ways. I will never know what parts of my personality, talents, or the way I see the world, are because of bipolar. Neither will I know what I would have been like had I never developed this illness. Some sufferers express they would never swap having bipolar for a life as an ordinary person. I imagine for them, the creative energy and intoxicating manias are worth the aftermath. I'm not someone who gets so much from bipolar that I would hate to be without it. Most of what I get is unpleasant. For me, bipolar is a burden and I would swap it for good health every day of the week. Having said this, I have no idea what I would be like without bipolar, so in truth, it is an impossible dilemma for me to answer.

However, there are silver linings. If I look at bipolar from the perspective of my soul, rather than outer success or ease of life, I can see value in the illness. Whilst casting a dark cloud over large parts of my adult life, bipolar has without doubt driven me to develop as a human being. It has opened my eyes to aspects of life I would never otherwise have known about.

I no longer believe my life on earth is about material success or achievement. For me it is about developing and growing as a human being. It is about friendship, laughter and love. Being kind to others and myself and leaving the world a better place than I found it. This means expanding love and compassion in myself and in the world. In this regard, bipolar has great value. By preventing me from doing what I wanted to do, I learned patience and humility. By presenting me with "unacceptable" situations, I learned acceptance. Through the suffering it delivered, I learned compassion and more understanding of other people's hardships.

Current medical opinion states bipolar can't be cured, which means I will probably take lithium for the rest of my days. On their own, neither lithium, meditation nor therapy could have led me to my peaceful state. It was only through a combination of the three that I have found a balance. I can't do many of the things I used to enjoy doing and I may never have a successful career in the traditional sense, but I appreciate the simple pleasures; the laughter, the crisp winter mornings, meals with my parents, lying in bed with my wife, hot chocolates with my stepson and teasing the people I love. I have, by the grace of the journey I travelled, befriended an illness I once feared, denied and hated.

From time to time, we all get rear-ended by life and its challenges can affect us in a variety of ways. Sometimes they lead to resentment; and at others they can be the making of us. Once the dust of a challenge has settled, a gift can reveal itself and we are able to find blessings within terrible events. The psychoanalyst Carl Jung believed the unconscious mind creates events in our lives to teach us lessons. These lessons can lead to higher levels of happiness. Sometimes they are painful because people and things we care about are taken from us, our defences are stripped and our soul laid bare. Yet, if we have the correct approach, these lessons can change us for the better. The false superficialities that life weaves around our personality are ripped away and a wisdom, presence and sense of humour are found in their place. The challenges bipolar has brought me have made me into a more rounded person, more appreciative of what I have and of the people around me.

My dance with this illness has been far from a graceful waltz. If I'm honest, it has been more like a break dance on speed, but it has taught me vital life lessons and for these I am grateful. Its challenges could have ended my marriage, but have in fact strengthened it. Most of the credit for this goes to my wife, who is an incredible person and has stood beside me no matter what. She has been a rock, holding our family together under enormous stress and strain. I attribute her patience and solidity to the deep well of love which exists within her, a well which gave her strength beyond what I could have ever imagined.

Once I began to recover, her perseverance and patience began to pay off. My appreciation for what she had done for me transformed into a deep devotion to her, which then evolved into a laughter and love filled relationship, with a depth neither of us have experienced before. My parents too have been unconditionally kind and loving. They have seen me at my worst, but have always been there for me consistently throughout my life.

Bipolar still encroaches on my life at times. I can't train or play sport; if I overexert myself, I get headaches and become dizzy and irritable. In the autumn, I have the tendency to hallucinate and drift towards psychosis. In winter, I sometimes lose my zest for life and slip into a mild depression. However, these situations are manageable and rarely last for more than a day or three. The rest of the time, I'm as happy as the proverbial pig in shit.

Finally, I would like to share a list of traits which have been developed or strengthened by the challenges bipolar has thrown my way. As I have mentioned before, if I could wave a magic wand and be healed of bipolar, I would wave it without a second's thought. I don't have such a wand, but I can choose to be grateful for the growth I have experienced because of having this illness. Part of being a human is facing up to the challenges which life throws at us. We may not desire them, but very few of us escape them. If we have the right approach, we let them bring out the best in us.

Confidence: When I was first ill, bipolar shattered my confidence, but it had been a boyish, cocky kind, not true confidence. Over time, I discovered a deeper inner strength and it became clear my mental health challenges had not broken me. In fact, they have made me stronger.

Courage: Courage is not an absence of fear, it is being afraid and doing the brave thing anyway. Bipolar took me to places I would never have wanted to go, but I survived and discovered an inner resilience I never knew I had.

Humility: I used to be arrogant, but now I would – with all due humility – describe myself as one of the humblest people in the world. Only joking! On a more serious note: I did suffer from arrogance, priding myself in being more intelligent and quick-witted than most. I judged others harshly and I didn't suffer fools gladly. There are few things more humbling than being battered by life and bipolar's battering went a long way towards destroying my arrogance.

Priorities: Although ambition can lead to great achievements, it doesn't usually bring happiness. In its nature ambition is dissatisfied with the *status quo*. By "failing" in critical areas, particularly in my career, I was given the opportunity to let go of the chains of ambition that had pushed me for as long as I can remember. Ambition in itself is not a bad thing, but my ambition was driven by low self-worth and a need to prove myself.

I can now be happy whilst having a life which I never aspired to have. I now know some of the simplest pleasures can be the most rewarding. I love riding my motorbike, giving talks, teaching meditation and doing repairs around the house. I don't need to climb Mount Everest or be a top sales trader to feel alive.

Peace: Ironically, I may be more peaceful because I have bipolar. The illness gave me a great incentive to put my energy into cultivating peace and spurred me towards finding my spiritual path. It gave me many good reasons to try to free myself from emotional suffering and the pain inflicted by my mind. Had life gone my way and I had been born with a steady mind, would I have sought out peace? Probably not.

Acceptance: By being forced to accept the unacceptable, I have learned to embrace life the way it is. By this I mean I have stopped fighting and begrudging the life I have been given. I have become better at going with the flow and being sensitive; not just to what I want to happen, but to what life wants to happen too.

Compassion: Through suffering, I have developed a depth of compassion for others I would never otherwise have done. I have learned that everyone has their challenges and their disappointments; and it is better to meet people with love and kindness than to judge them. Without bipolar I would have had no idea about what a person with mental illness goes through and wouldn't be able to relate to them in the way I do now.

I still sometimes have suicidal thoughts, but they don't bother me in the way they used to. I have learned to ignore them and when I do, they lose their power. Interestingly, I can have suicidal thoughts and be at peace at the same time. Something I never knew was possible.

Bipolar has taken me to the limits of my strength and endurance, causing me to feel broken and separate from everyone I know. Now, despite this illness, I lead an interesting and fulfilling life. I am more content than I have ever been. I have done what I thought would be impossible. Not only have I befriended bipolar, but I have become better friends with myself too.

These days my life revolves around my family and part-time work as a writer, speaker and coach. On a normal day, I wake up with a happy anticipation of what the day may bring. Then I look over to my right and there is my lovely wife snoozing beside me. I stroll into the kitchen in our cosy little flat and make us a cup of tea, appreciating what I have more than ever.

Maybe I will spend the day writing or give a talk. If the weather is good, I will take a ride on my motorbike. Whatever I do, I will most likely enjoy it, accompanied by a peaceful and happy presence that gives me such stability. I don't often look back at my more painful episodes, but if I went back in time six years, I would never have said the words I am about to write.

"It's good to be alive. Life is good."

TO THE READER

Thank you for reading this book. If you enjoyed it, please tell your friends about it. Please also leave a review on Amazon. I read all the reviews and they help me to get the message out there.

THANK YOU

Hiranya Seligman, Elizabeth Seligman, Richard Seligman, James Hicks, David Murray, Tone Fagerli, Liz Palm, Alison Gordon and Sarah Irwin

For giving so much of your time and energy in helping me with this book.

THE AUTHOR

Oliver is a writer, inspirational speaker and coach. If you are interested in contacting him, he can be found on
www.befriendingbipolar.co.uk

Oliver is the author of two other books, "The Broker who broke free" and "No Rest for the Wicked." He also has his own YouTube channel called Befriending Bipolar

REFERENCES

Introduction:

[1] Bipolar disorder is not curable, but there are many treatments and strategies that a person can use to manage their symptoms: Medical News Today.

[2] As many as one in five patients with bipolar disorder completes suicide (The United States National Institute of Mental Health).

[3] Inspired by The Johns Hopkins Psychiatric Guide.

[4] Inspired by The United States National Institute of Mental Health.

[5] More than two-thirds of people with bipolar disorder have at least one close relative with the illness or with major depression, indicating that the disease has a heritable component. (National Institute of Mental Health)

[6] Monica Aas, Chantal Henry, Ole A. Andreassen, Frank Belliver, Ingrid Melle and Bruno Etain. The role of childhood trauma in bipolar disorders. Published in *International Journal of Bipolar Disorders*, January 2016.

[7] The United States National Institute of Mental Health.

Chapter 2:

[8] The Mental Health Foundation (UK).

[9] Trials at the Aintree University Hospital in 2018 showed that flexible visiting hours improved patient outcomes (UK National Health Service website).

Chapter 3:

[10] Emanuel Severus, Willem A. Nolen & Michael Bauer. Lithium: The best current treatment for the well-informed bipolar patient. Published in *Bipolar Disorders Volume 23, Issue 1*, February 2021.

[11] Leonardo Tondo, Martin Alda, Michael Bauer, Veerle Bergink, Paul Grof, Tomas Hajek, Ute Lweitka, Rasmus W. Licht, Mirko Manchia, Bruno Muller-Oerlinghausen, Rene E. Nielsen, Marylou Selo, Christian Simhandl & Ross J. Baldessarini. Clinical use of lithium salts: guide for users and prescribers. Published in *International Journal of Bipolar Disorders,* July 2019.

[12] Stuppes and colleagues (1991) found that over 50% of manic episodes occurred 3 months after stopping lithium.

Chapter 4:

[13] Verywellmind.com (a partner of The Cleveland Clinic, the number two rated hospital in the United States).

Chapter 5:

[14] Harvard Health Publishing; Harvard Medical School.

[15] Leonardo Tondo, Gustavo H. Vazquez & Ross J. Baldessarini. Depression and mania in bipolar disorder. *Journal of Current Neuropharmacology,* April 2017.

Chapter 6:

[16] The Encyclopedia Brittanica.

[17] Dr. Fred Luskin, Professor at the Institute of Transpersonal Psychology, Stanford University.

Chapter 9:

[18] Office of National Statistics.

[19] As many as one in five patients with bipolar disorder completes suicide. (The United States National Institute of Mental Health).

Chapter 10:

[20] Healthgrades.com

Chapter 11:

[21] Citizens Commission on Human Rights International: The Mental health industry watchdog.

Chapter 13:

[22] For the typical male or female aged 25 to 45 years with bipolar disorder, the remaining life expectancy is decreased by 12 to 8.7 years and 10.6 to 8.3 years respectively. Lars Vedel Kessing, Eleni Vradi and Per Kragh Andersen. Life expectancy in bipolar disorder. Published in *Bipolar Disorders: An International Journal of Psychiatry and Neurosciences*, August 2015.

Chapter 14:

[23] Christoffer van Tulleken, Michael Tipton, Heather Massey and C Mark Harper. Open water swimming as a treatment for major depressive disorder. Published in *British Medical Journal Case Reports*. 2018

[24] Alexandra K. Gould & Louisa G. Sylvia. The role of sleep in bipolar disorder. Published in *Nature and Science of Sleep Journal*. June 2016.

[25] I use a product from Iristech.com.

[26] Willa Goodfellow, bestselling author of Prozac Monologues: A Voice from the Edge.

[27] Positive news (www.positive.news) and Future Crunch (futurecrunch.com).

[28] For more on this, read The Polyvagal Theory by Stephen Porges.

Chapter 15:

[29] The meditation that I have practiced for the last twenty years is called Ascension (www.thebrightpath.com).

[30] The National Science Foundation (2005).

Printed in Great Britain
by Amazon